P9-DWX-972

Twayne's English Authors Series

Sylvia E. Bowman, *Editor*

INDIANA UNIVERSITY

Charles Robert Maturin

 *156*

Charles Robert Maturin

By DALE KRAMER

University of Illinois

Twayne Publishers, Inc. : : New York

Copyright © 1973 by Twayne Publishers, Inc.

All Rights Reserved

Library of Congress Catalog Card Number: 72–13379

PR
4987
· M7
Z 75

ISBN 0–8057–1382–4

MANUFACTURED IN THE UNITED STATES OF AMERICA

66901

Preface

Charles Maturin's *Melmoth the Wanderer* is generally acknowledged the masterpiece of the Gothic novels, but his other novels and his plays are less widely known. However, his total output comprises a major contribution to early nineteenth-century English literature, and this study attempts to acquaint the reader with the quality of his works, his personality, and the conditions under which he worked.

The proportions for the individual parts of this book are determined essentially by the material, but I do not suggest my opinion of the relative value of Maturin's works by the amount of space I give to them. The length of chapters reflects sometimes the necessity to communicate the flavor of a complicated story, such as *Fatal Revenge;* and sometimes the length is required to explain all the matters of interest that a book contains despite the undistinguished literary quality of the book itself, such as *The Albigenses.* Maturin's miscellaneous works—two poems, two essays, and the sermons—are discussed in relevant contexts rather than in separate chapters. These miscellanea have little intrinsic value.

A basic concern in the book is to relate Maturin to Gothicism, the literary mode that permitted a release of his imaginative fantasies. I discuss Gothicism twice, once to explain its influence on the novel and once to explain its influence on the drama. In most respects, of course, Gothic fiction and drama closely resemble each other; but Maturin's use of conventions appropriate to each genre, and his handling of the Gothic villain are different enough in the two genres to warrant separate consideration.

The history of Gothicism is a cloudy and quite complex one. Rather than attempt to discuss all of the complexities or to argue the numerous moot points concerning influences, causes, authors' philosophies, and so forth, I have decided, since these sections are intended primarily as introductions to Maturin's Gothic works, to put forth as succinctly as possible the main outline of the development of Gothicism. Much of this outline is a synthesis of conflicting theories. I indicate both Maturin's innovations and imitations in the Gothic mode, especially concerning the plays, which have received practically no detailed esthetic or generic analysis. I do not attempt to give in any full way all of the influences upon Maturin nor to indicate all of his borrowings. As was customary in his time, he borrowed heavily without acknowledgment. I do discuss matters of indebtedness that have not been previously identified or explained, such as the parallels between Sydney Owenson's *Wild Irish Girl* and Maturin's *Milesian Chief,* an indebtedness long recognized but never investigated.

This study is indebted to the University of Illinois Library, especially to Miss Alma De Jordy of the acquisitions department for obtaining materials at my request that the library's extensive holdings did not already contain. Ronald Epple was of invaluable help in scanning early nineteenth-century periodicals for reviews of Maturin's works, many of which had not been cited by previous writers on Maturin. My wife Cheris Kramer has offered suggestions for improvement of the writing during the entire development of the manuscript. Financial assistance has been given by the University of Illinois Graduate College and by the American Philosophical Society.

Canon R. H. Dowse, Rector of St. Peter's Church in Dublin, was helpful in explaining the records of his church, of which Maturin was curate for many years. For assistance in biographical research, I am grateful to Miss P. Maturin of Belfast; the Reverend J. Charles Combe of Belfast; the Public Records Offices in Dublin and London; and to Miss G. Willis, librarian of the Representative Church Body of the Anglican Church of Ireland. Dr. James Corson, the honorary librarian of Abbotsford, and Mrs. Patricia Maxwell-Scott assisted my examination of the unpublished manuscript of Maturin's *Bertram*. The National Library of Scotland and Mr. John Murray of London have allowed me to examine and to quote from Maturin's unpublished correspondence.

DALE KRAMER

University of Illinois

Contents

Chronology

1780   Charles Maturin born in Dublin, September 25.

1800   Graduated from Trinity College, Dublin.

1803   Ordained in the Anglican Church of Ireland; became curate at Loughrea, a rural parish, but evidently spent little time there, staying most of the time at Cloghan Castle in western Ireland, where no doubt the scenes for *Wild Irish Boy* and *The Milesian Chief* had their inspiration.

1803   Married to Henrietta Kingsbury in October.

1805   Became curate at St. Peter's parish, Dublin; remained at this post until he died.

1807   *Fatal Revenge* published, under the pseudonym of Dennis Jasper Murphy.

1808   *The Wild Irish Boy.*

1809   Father lost position as one of the Clerks of the Road in the Irish General Post Office on charge of malfeasance, though a board of enquiry later found him to be innocent of the charges. Maturin now needed to write for money; and he tutored pupils to prepare them for the university.

1810   Sir Walter Scott reviewed *Fatal Revenge;* Maturin opened their correspondence in 1812.

1812   *The Milesian Chief,* the first novel which Maturin sold outright, for £80.

1813   *Bertram* written.

1815   The Waterloo prize poem.

1816   *Bertram* produced and published in London. Maturin's greatest financial success; but most of the money went to his brother's creditors.

1817   *Manuel.*

1818   *Women; or, Pour et Contre.*

1819   *Fredolfo.*

1819   *Sermons.*

1820   *Melmoth the Wanderer.*

1821   *Universe, a Poem*—actually written by James Wills.

1824   *The Albigenses.*

1824   *Five Sermons of the Errors of the Roman Catholic Church.*

1824   Maturin died in Dublin, October 30; buried in the churchyard of St. Peter's.

1830   Production in Dublin of *Osmyn, the Renegade; or, The Siege of Salerno.* Never published in its entirety; written sometime after 1817 and before 1821.

CHAPTER 1

Introduction

L ITTLE concrete information about Charles Maturin's life is available to the student of his works. In the course of writing this book I have uncovered a fair amount of previously unknown detail, but much of it is trivial and none is deeply revelatory of his character. The essential matters have long been known. He was born into a comfortable family descended from a French Huguenot priest who fled France after the Edict of Nantes during the reign of Louis XIV. Maturin attended Trinity College in Dublin, married Henrietta Kingsbury on October 25, 1803, took orders in the Established Church, and served as one of the poorly paid curates of St. Peter's in Dublin from 1805 until the end of his life.

Still, elements of Maturin's life suggest something of the nature of his literary distinctiveness. In telling the story about his French ancestor, Maturin emphasized two points: that his ancestor had been found as a baby by a French noblewoman on the Rue des Mathurines in Paris (thus his name) and that his religious persecution at the hands of Catholics had included twenty-six years in the Bastille. Reveling in such a pedigree, for which he is the sole authority, is one of the simpler manifestations of Maturin's love of the exotic and of his mania concerning Catholic cruelty. The posthumously published "Leixlip Castle" recounts another romantic story, which he insisted in a preface had actually occurred, about one of his ancestors who dealt in necromancy.

Maturin was denied preferment in the Irish Church because of his eccentricity; indeed, many Dublin citizens thought him insane. His unstable and paranoid personality helps account for the melodramatic bases of his plots as well as for the extremes of Gothic horror he was inclined to exploit for its own sake. But, while tongues wagged of his madness, his insatiable appetite for dancing, and his eagerness for literary fame, he earned the praises of his parishioners for the performance of his duties;[1] and, in an age famous for immorality, his reputation was unstained. He labored to establish a school at the same time he was writing novels and carrying out his parish duties.[2] A fervent nationalist and opponent of the Act of Union which in 1801 brought Ireland under England's total control through the guise of offering economic and political stability, his fondness for Irish tradition and affection for the miserable Irish masses account for the sense of concreteness of realized life in his novels, especially in his Irish novels but also in important sections of *Melmoth the Wanderer.*

Though Maturin lived all of his life in Dublin, he was not without literary counsel and assistance in the more bustling outer world. His famous friendship with Sir Walter Scott was initiated by Maturin when he learned that Scott had authored an anonymous review praising *Fatal Revenge.*[3] He wrote to Scott, modestly enough at first, and the generous Scott boosted Maturin's career on several occasions by his influence and business contacts. He warmly recommended Maturin's plays to London producers, and he helped arrange the publication of Maturin's last three novels by Constable & Company, the Edinburgh publishing firm which published Scott's novels. Another literary friendship was with Alaric Watts, the theatrical manager and journalist who superintended the London production of Maturin's play *Fredolfo.*

Watts appeared too late in Maturin's career to be of great help; and, in any case, the value of such friendships depends on a man's ability to move beyond them to an independent position. This movement Maturin was unable to accomplish. His great chance came when he was invited to come to London on the success of *Bertram;* but for reasons that are not entirely clear, Maturin's days as a literary lion were short-lived and never repeated. His letters to John Murray after his return to Dublin suggest that Maturin possessed a petulant and querulous character that took affront at the casualness of his reception: "I am infinitely obliged by your having the goodness to assure me the impression I made was favourable, but confess I want all the Evidence of your testimony to prove it—I went over, not expecting much, and came back receiving nothing—not even common civility, which in *Certain quarters* I surely *was intitled* to as an *invited stranger*—"[4]

Indeed, there is scarcely a letter by Maturin that does not contain a lament about his lot, indicating a personality that would not please in a brief personal acquaintance. Maturin's letters to Constable—self-pitying, pleading, embarrassingly servile and desperate—show what a trial he could be in business dealings. Scott had to exert all his influence to keep Archibald Constable from dumping Maturin from the firm's authors because of a nearly two-year delay by Maturin in finishing *Melmoth.*

Maturin's work was known in literary circles after the publication of *Fatal Revenge* in 1807; but his only popular success was with *Bertram,* and the profits of that play largely went toward paying the debts of a person—possibly his brother—for whom Maturin had gone security and who had immediately declared bankruptcy.[5] Maturin possessed a brilliant literary orginality; but his times had no form he could express himself in to his best advantage. His style is close to that of Thomas De Quincey's introspective essays, but Maturin could not maintain his intensity and passion over many pages at a time. His moods vary widely in an extended narrative; therefore, sentimental and Gothic fiction seemed to offer the most natural form for his ideas. He spent his life looking for a form he could imitate profitably, trying Gothic fiction and drama, tales of Irish life, and historical fiction in turn and in combination.

But he certainly did not write merely for money, despite his humble admissions in his prefaces of the meanness of his literary ambitions and his protestations in his letters to Scott that he would do literally anything not demeaning to a gentleman in order to support his family, including entering business or government. Before the entire Maturin family was thrown into desperate poverty by his father's loss of his government post in 1809, Maturin had published two novels at his own expense. And he might well have gained church preferment if he had not tarnished his reputation with play- and novel-writing, despite his unconventionality and his doctrinal differences with his Dublin superiors.[6] His family had held several high positions in the Anglican Church in Ireland; for example, his grandfather had been Dean of St. Patrick's (succeeding Jonathan Swift); and his wife's brother was a fast-rising clergyman who became the Archdeacon of Killala. Clearly, Maturin simply felt more inclined to literary efforts than to clerical, and the effect of his father's encouragement of his poetry and parlor theatrical productions when he was a youth overbalanced the attractiveness of professional advancement.

A good bit of Maturin's impetus to write is comprised by three contemporary forces discussed later. Gothicism and anti-

Catholicism dominate the works on which his fame rests; Irish nationalism provides subject matter for the two minor novels that followed *Fatal Revenge*. He is at his most original in *Melmoth*, his only work that permits all three forces to come together in one context. Also, the general pervading spirit of Romanticism was a major influence upon his mind-set, but it is not one that can be simply described.[7]

Maturin must also have possessed a psychological imbalance that could find satisfactory expression only in the extravagances of Gothicism, although causes for such an imbalance cannot be located in what few facts are known about the life of a pampered and admired younger son who enjoyed an indolent college career studded with academic awards and an esteemed, if small, scholarship. The financial failure of *Fatal Revenge* informed him in 1807 that Gothic fiction was not the highroad to wealth, but he refused to benefit from the knowledge later when money was a more pressing issue. Every novel after *Fatal Revenge* has characteristic Gothic elements—exotic plots, motiveless villains, delicate sketchings of mental torment, remarkable physical attributes of the major male protagonists, and atmospheric details and landscape that color the action. Even after he had been reminded of the risks by the failure of his last two Gothic plays, Maturin returned to the Gothic mode in *Melmoth the Wanderer* as the form best able to accommodate his most forceful esthetic and religious ideas.

I *Gothicism*

Although not all of Maturin's productions can be generically classified as "Gothic," all of his works contain features or scenes common to Gothicism, making clear how congenial to his taste and talents were Gothic materials. His best works are his Gothic works; and he is remembered only for his Gothic works, especially for *Melmoth the Wanderer* by all well-read students of literature; for *Bertram* by historians of English drama; and for *Fatal Revenge* by devotees of Gothicism. All three are excellent examples of Gothic writing, though only *Melmoth* has the balance and the assured ease of variety that marks the literary work whose subject matter accords totally with the writer's sense of style.

Gothicism, as do literary modes like Realism and mysticism, has its beginnings as far back as the original impulse to tell stories. Evocations of fear or suspense, references to the supernatural, the causal relationship between setting and atmosphere—these are the essential foundations of the Gothic mode. But modes crystallize at some point in history, and the crystallization of the Gothic spirit essentially began in the Renaissance. The drama of Shakespeare with the witches in *Macbeth,* the guilt-haunted castle of Elsinore in *Hamlet,* the villainous figures of Iago, Richard III, and King Claudius—employs characteristics that became the dominant motifs in Gothic literature: supernaturalism, architectural amplification of human doubts and fears, and the wily, inscrutable villain. Other Elizabethan dramatists, such as Philip Massinger and John Ford, anticipate the Gothicists' obsession with revenge and incest.

The Gothic spirit, which in part is one of rebellion and an urge to freedom, occurs with a subsidiary emphasis in post-Puritan art forms such as the heroic drama, which eschews restraint on rhetoric and metaphor. But even a Puritan work such as John Milton's *Paradise Lost* reflects this spirit. Satan is nearly an archetypal Gothic villain. Obsessed with his guilt and failure, at the same time he bitterly undercuts the virtue and happiness of the innocent.

But the eighteenth century, with its paradoxical mystique of reason, provided the context for the most widely manifested upsurge of the Gothic spirit. Running parallel through the entire century, but with opposite biases, were the belief that only the rational exercise of intelligence held man above the chaos of mere animalism and the enthusiasms of demagogues, and the belief that life lived strictly according to rational precepts was cut off from many worthwhile and valid experiences. The first belief is demonstrated in the works of the great Augustans, Alexander Pope ("Essay on Man") and Samuel Johnson (*Lives of the Poets*) in particular. This typifies the eighteenth century in modern popular descriptions, which project the century as a Classical age, of commonsensical reasoning and quiet emotions.

The second belief, however, is as pervasive as the first; it appears in the dominant mood of the century, melancholy, which affects even Pope ("Eloisa to Abelard") and Johnson ("The Vanity of Human Wishes") in a way that denies the separability of the two beliefs. Distillation of this mood of melancholy is in the work of an Oxford don, Thomas Gray, whose "Elegy Written in a Country

Churchyard" evokes superstitious piety and the supremacy of humble virtue that are entirely akin to the ultimate moral message of the Gothic novel. The consanguinity of the two beliefs is dramatically evident in Edmund Burke's *On the Sublime* (1757). The supreme conservative thinker and Classical theorist of the century, Burke points out that mysteriousness, suggestions of superstitious loathings, indefinite and irregular landscapes, and architectural ruins create an emotion of sublimity appropriate to themes of grandeur. Burke's work, then, is the epitome of the eighteenth-century paradox: a rationalistic explanation of and justification for Romantic excess.

A similar quality of ineluctable paradox operates throughout the Gothic movement and is the source of much of the esthetic tension in its literature. Burke's theorizing only formalizes what other writers intuited and employed in imaginative works. Almost every major element in the Gothic novel has inherent contradictions. The use of nature is perhaps the best case in point. Like the sentimental novelists in general, Gothic writers lauded peaceful and serene rural scenes as quasi-religious settings for the exercise of virtue. The sentimentalists asserted that social institutions and sophistication were evil—if not in themselves (and they usually were), then in their blinding one's eyes to proper humility, selfhood, and disinterestedness. But for the Gothicists nature also contained dynamism and raw energy—projected most obviously in storm scenes amidst mountains or isolated seasides—that were the equivalents for the forcefulness, pride, and ruthlessness that were as much parts of mankind's makeup as was a love of security and peace. The usual employment of this paradox is to isolate the virtuous heroine in a mountain castle, where the threats of the villain are reinforced by terrific winds and thunders.

An antiquarian interest in the past, especially in medieval accouterments such as armor, and in Gothic architecture, became more intense through the century. The Gothic period of architecture had lasted from the twelfth to the sixteenth century and in England had been utilized mainly in ecclesiastical buildings. Many of these had been destroyed by Henry VIII in his confiscation of church lands and dissolution of the monasteries. Castles fell into ruins as titles lapsed and as methods of warfare changed. As a result, to Englishmen's minds, Gothic architecture came to be associated with the derelict buildings of a defunct feudal and priestly society, although new buildings imitating the Gothic style were still being built and although artificial "ruins" were being constructed by landscape gardeners to form vistas. This association, along with the belief that architectural ruins encouraged mental gloom, helps to account for two of the more noticeable characteristics of the Gothic novel: the anachronistic disrepair of castles that at the projected time of the stories would have been recently built, and the employment of religious communities as a major factor in the persecution of the victims.

Gothic novelists are commonly supposed to be anti-Catholic; and some, such as Maturin, actually did have objections to Catholic doctrine.[8] But probably the more important reason writers depicted the Catholic church as villainous was its position of power and thus its potential for being oppressive, in the medieval society which the Gothic novel reconstructs. Another important reason is that virtually no one in England, including the novelists themselves, had firm knowledge of actual practices in medieval ecclesiastical societies.[9] Therefore, the meanest canards could be perpetrated without fear of contradiction; equally important, practices could be inaccurately described in ways that increased the atmosphere of fear and mystery. Descriptions of midnight processions of nuns, for example, were popular for their effect. Imaginations of the novelists were especially activated by the secret interrogative practices of the Inquisition[10] and by the rigorous discipline of the monasteries. Many Gothic writers did not know the difference between monks and priests; and several took it for granted that convents and monasteries would be connected by subterranean passages, no matter how many miles separated them—not for lascivious intercourse between the monks and nuns, but to further the diabolic oppression of naïve and virtuous members of the communities.

The English nation had short tolerance for Catholicism, remembering the threat to the stability of their society posed by the Stuart claim to the throne, which, though routed in the 1745 defeat of Bonnie Prince Charlie's armies, was feared until the end of the century, when revolutionary and Bonapartist threats from France effaced the remnants of suspicion concerning the Stuarts. This fear of Catholicism permitted the harsh "penal code" of Ireland that virtually dispossessed the four-fifths of the island's population that were Catholic and made their situation little better than that of serfs. Thus, even the writers who had no personal bias realized they could exploit Gothic conventions concerning Catholicism without fear of public disfavor. Even the English Catholics raised few objections to the misrepresentations of the practices of their church in medieval times; and Maturin's personal observation of humane Catholicism in Ireland did not prevent his aggrandizing its supposed inhumanity in Italy and in Spain.

But the Gothic novel is the result of more sweeping forces than any of those described so far. The movement was too widespread to permit us to look only to England or to a single monolithic religion for its sources. It was a phenomenon of Western Europe, even of Western civilization. The larger cause was a natural psychological reaction to a socio-political situation, the individual appeal being indissolubly linked to the mass appeal. The Gothic novel is the literary expression of the reaction against the repressions and boundaries of neo-Classical thought and conservative politics. The reaction accommodated the rise of Rousseauism and the subsequent thrust toward democracy and anarchy in European political organization. Whether the writers themselves were politically conservative or revolutionary,[11] their works in most respects reflect and substantiate the revolutionary undercurrent, most importantly in their support of emotions and in enlarging the scope of imagination to include a spiritual level, but also in the thematic-moral implications in the contours of the novels' actions.

It is impossible to avoid connecting the Reign of Terror of the French Revolution and the Gothic novel. Mobs in "Monk" Lewis' and Maturin's novels are seen to be dispensing a basic justice when they tear to pieces a vindictive and murderous prioress and a parricide, thereby implying a sympathy with the procedures of Isidore Maximilien de Robespierre and his Committee of Public Safety that either Lewis or Maturin would have sincerely refused to acknowledge as his considered opinion. In responding to the spirit of the age as artists, they went beyond their conservative intellectual positions as men in an existing society.

II   Gothic Character Types

A characteristic of Gothicism is its use of the exotic and distant past for a setting, but this employment is not historical. With rare exception, the Gothic novelists were no more trustworthy with historical facts than with religious usages. They used known facts loosely and created "historical" circumstances when the need arose. Moreover, the Gothicists made no pretense to re-create a medieval perspective upon the action; rather, they transported eighteenth-century personality types and moral standards to the medieval setting.

The Gothic hero and heroine are eighteenth-century ideals, both directly taken from the popular sentimental novels. The hero is usually a nonentity and is frequently absent from the action altogether, for the center of the plot is the villain's persecution of the heroine. The hero is fearless; and, while he can be tempted from virtue, he always chastises himself and becomes worthy finally to wed the heroine. (Valancourt in Ann Radcliffe's *The Mysteries of Udolpho* provides an example of the type: his grief at the thought that his beloved Emily is dead leads him to a temporary dissipation in Paris.) The heroine faints readily at evidences of ghosts but fearlessly reads moldy manuscripts at midnight and explores long-forgotten passageways with only a frightened maid to accompany her, and she often is alone. The subsidiary character roles are also of eighteenth-century derivation rather than medieval. Even chivalric knights speak of love with the accents of sentimental domesticity rather than those of the "religion" of courtly amorality of Chrétien de Troyes or Andreas Cappelanus' *De Arte Honeste Amandi.*

One principal kind of Gothic character does not come from the eighteenth century, however. He is timeless, though, as I have said, his ancestors figure largely in Elizabethan and heroic drama. This character is the Gothic villain. Larger than reality, unrestrained by common ideas of decency and humaneness, unable and usually unwilling to reorient his life though tortured by the sense of his own evilness, the Gothic villain is an endlessly fascinating psychological study, and he is the most distinctive feature of the Gothic novel. Without him, and the mood he instills, the stories would be more accurately defined as pseudo-historical romances, as ghost tales, or as scenic narratives.

The Gothic villain expresses the rejection of restraint that civilizations place on man's natural self-expression, and he often does so with such fantastic behavior that verisimilitude can be only a partial test of the author's success. He mocks man-made law, ignores locks on doors and prisons in which men may try to place him, and takes sadistic pleasure in tormenting people who stand between him and success—whether "success" be wealth, seduction of a beautiful woman, establishment of a family dynasty, or destruction of an enemy. What is remarkable about the Gothic villain is that—totally unsympathetic in his actions—he attracts readers at a subliminal level, one deeper than consciousness. This quality has led critics to approximate the Gothic villain with the Freudian "id": the raw impulse to power and self-gratification, the projections of repressed dreams of the author—and, by extension, the impulses and projections of the society. The villain expresses certain of society's values in ways that society by self-censorship prohibits itself from condoning.

Perhaps the widest-known Gothic villain is Heathcliff of Emily Brontë's *Wuthering Heights,* whose cruelty and destructiveness are amoral. Modern criticism, in an attempt to understand Brontë's evident condonation of Heathcliff, thinks that he represents one of the prime forces of energy in the universe. The Gothic villain has basic similarities to the antihero of modern American fiction: both reject society's ostensible and hypocritical standards and have erected their own code of conduct. The differences are the degree of cruelty in the Gothic villain and the despair that dominates his mental attitude. Unlike the modern antihero, the Gothic villain recognizes the power of God and the immutability of divine law. He knows that his independent behavior dooms him, and he accepts the justice of his fate.

III   *Landmarks in Gothic Fiction*

The term "Gothic" had a common currency throughout the eighteenth century as a term meaning old and uncouth and as an architectural term used without clear distinction to refer either to the "old" Gothic (Romanesque, ponderous, depressing, with heavy masses) or to the "new" Gothic (ornamental, elaborate structures of separate parts and obtrusive details). But the full potentialities of the concept went unrealized until Horace Walpole, the son of the former prime minister, soured against public life and retreated to Twickenham, where he built a fake Gothic mansion, with suits of armor, a winding staircase, and stained-glass windows. In these surroundings he experienced tremendous dreams. One of these dreams, of a huge hand in armor, so excited his imagination that he wrote in two months *The Castle of Otranto* (1765 [1764]), subtitled *A Gothic Story.*

Walpole's story contains a ghost capable both of expanding itself and of dismembering itself, portraits which step down from their frames, and a usurping nobleman who wishes to marry the fiancée of his mysteriously murdered son in order to ensure an heir to his fraudulent title. Though utterly fantastic, the tale aroused great enthusiasm. From the perspective of time, we can see this early Gothic craze as a novelty which gave exotic impetus to the interest in weather and ruins that James Thomson (*The Seasons*) and the graveyard poets—Gray, Robert Blair, Edward Young—had been musing on for years. The grandiosity of *Otranto* taps the legendary heroism of a past Romantic culture that James Macpherson's *Ossian* (1760–63) had exploited, and the antiquarianism that Thomas Percy's *Reliques of Ancient English Poetry* (1765) appealed to in the same year as *Otranto.*

Oddly, there were no imitators of Walpole's success until Clara Reeve, outraged by Walpole's violations of common sense, wrote *The Old English Baron* in 1777 (originally entitled *The Champion of Virtue: A Gothic Story*). Reeve does have a ghost, but limits its activities to groaning and pointing. Walpole scornfully said that Miss Reeve evidently did not think that a "tame" ghost would violate probability. After Reeve, other novelists attempted to combine fearful situations and exotic historical backgrounds. But the genre stagnated with dull-minded repetition of devices intended to astonish.

Then Ann Radcliffe improved upon historical Gothicism in a series of novels in which she perfected her new form, ratiocinative Gothicism, and introduced features that influenced the development of prose fiction. Borrowing from Walpole and Reeve, she delighted in innumerable mysterious circumstances—ghostly voices, discoveries of skeletons in trunks and recesses in walls, manuscripts read in flickering candlelight, and nocturnal visits to haunted chambers.

But, unlike Walpole, whose ghosts were real and whose superstitions defined effective forces, Radcliffe ingeniously rationalizes every supernatural or mysterious element in her books. Perhaps the most striking deflation concerns the inexpressibly horrible object hidden by the drapery in a room in *The Mysteries of Udolpho* that is usually locked. Emily, the heroine who is held in the castle against her wishes, shudders whenever she recalls what she saw upon once drawing back the drapery. Only near the end of the novel does Radcliffe reveal that the object is a wax figure representing a partially decomposed body, placed in the room generations before at the order of a confessor to remind a former owner of the castle of his own inevitable end. The horrified Emily had not looked long enough to notice that the "body" was not real. Radcliffe's manner of explaining away horror and ghosts attracted both praise and criticism. Intelligent men now could enjoy fearful situations without feeling insulted by assumptions of the reality of ghosts; and novels became challenging puzzles to unravel before the author revealed the subterfuges. On the other hand, critics said that the use of shoddy tricks made it unbearable to read a Radcliffe novel more than once.

But her novels are not just clever deceptions. It is more relevant that she was the first novelist to use landscape and atmosphere poetically; she creates fear without resorting to the absurdities of Walpole's followers or the excesses of later Gothicists. Actual blood seldom enters a Radcliffe story. The gloom and fear of Emily in *Udolpho* are justified by the isolated situation of the massive castle, the wildness and grandeur of the Italian scenery, the darkness of the endless corridors, and the threatening behavior of the villain Montoni. The possibility of ghosts is an added factor, not an indispensable one. Radcliffe's delicacy in sketching moods and scenes makes her style the most polished of any of the Gothic school. She also contributed to the formation of the Gothic villain. Montoni is cruel and vindictive; he marries Lucy's aunt and wears down her nerves to cause her death and thereby benefit from her wealth without actually committing murder. More particularly, Schedoni in *The Italian* (1797) is the archetypal monkish villain. Profligate and hypocritical, unfeeling and implacable (until his paternal feelings are awakened), he also seems to possess abnormal physical powers. Schemoli in Maturin's *Fatal Revenge* is modeled directly on Schedoni.

Schedoni, however, was not an entirely original creation. The most notorious name in English Gothicism is that of Matthew Gregory Lewis, better known as "Monk" Lewis after the name of his literary monument, *The Monk* (1796). The protagonist-villain of *The Monk,* Ambrosius, is in some respects more grotesque than Schedoni, and he furnished Mrs. Radcliffe some hints when she came to limn the corruption of her own monk. Ambrosius is seduced from his life of saintly monastic austerity by Matilda, a voluptuous woman—at the end of the novel transformed into an agent of Satan—who disguises herself as a monk. Quickly wearying of Matilda, Ambrosius perfidiously lusts for Antonia, a youthful virgin who attends his sermons. Matilda's necromantic knowledge furnishes him with a drug that creates a state resembling death (an idea borrowed from *Romeo and Juliet*). When Antonia awakes in her tomb in the company of moldering corpses, Ambrosius is waiting. Despite her entreaties, he rapes her; and, to prevent her revealing his crime, he stabs her. Just before his own death at the hands of a triumphant Satan, Ambrosius learns that Antonia was his sister and that Antonia's mother, whom he had suffocated in an earlier attempt on Antonia's honor, was his own mother.

The restraint and artistic tact that distinguish Mrs. Radcliffe's work held no place in the credo of Lewis, who offers fulsome descriptions of rotting corpses, the thunderous shuddering of earth and the sulfurous fumes that attend the appearance of Satan, incarceration in reptile-filled dungeons, vengeful mobs attacking their victims, kisses by the specter of an unburied nun, the dankness and stifling atmosphere of subterranean chambers, and the odors of corruption in burial rooms. Lewis' *The Monk* was one result of the outbreak of the *Schauer-Romantik* ("horror-romanticism"), a phenomenon that spread rapidly among German, French, and English writers and whose emphasis on revolting details is at once the decadence of Gothicism and the most probable reason for the eventual demise of the craze for it. Lewis' detailed tracing of the progress of Ambrosius' emotions of concupiscence—from initial desire to uncontrollable lust to post-coitus loathing of the love partner—caused a storm of protest on the book's publication. It is perhaps needless to say that in comparison to descriptions of sexual activities in modern fiction, Lewis' are reasonably decorous; and undeniably they increase the sense of revulsion toward a state of society that permits privileged exploitation of the innocent. Ambrosius' sexual domination of Antonia amid the fetidness of the catacomb is unforgettable as a political metaphor, just as the linking of transient sensual pleasure with the immutable fact of physical death makes an unforgettable religious metaphor.

The most formative early Gothic novelists are Walpole, Radcliffe, and Lewis, but other novelists also enlarged the genre. In particular, William Godwin in his *St. Leon* (1799) and *Caleb*

Williams (1794) suggested a depth of intellectualization lacking in previous novelists.[12] Rejecting gross supernaturalism and skeptical of all existing philosophical systems but his own, Godwin suggests that mental obsessions alone can drive men to awful deeds. The subtitle of *Caleb Williams* is *Things as They Are,* and the relentless pursuit of Caleb by the wealthy Falkland reveals Godwin's concept of class oppression. *St. Leon* is based on a conception of the Wandering Jew theme similar to that which Maturin drew upon as a starting point for *Melmoth the Wanderer;* and, what is more characteristic of Godwin, the protagonist St. Leon is forced by experience to realize that extraordinary powers are more of a curse than a blessing in a conservative society.

Arguments as to the high point of the Gothic movement in England, and as to the "end" of the movement, cannot be settled, any more than any such ambiguous matters can be. Judging from periodical reviews, the high point seems to have been Radcliffe's *The Mysteries of Udolpho* and *The Italian.* Reviewers were generous in praise of Mrs. Radcliffe's effectiveness in creating emotion without offending sensibilities. Lewis' excesses, on the other hand, were instantly attacked, and the attack was carried over to other Gothic novelists. The common tone of reviews is ironic astonishment that still another account of spiritual phenomena had been produced. (Maturin himself never had a totally receptive press. Even Walter Scott's review of *Fatal Revenge* suggests that the pseudonymous author employ his talents in a different genre than the Gothic tale, a suggestion repeated as a matter of course in later years by reviewers who had the warmest regard for Maturin's abilities.) But the continued success of stage Gothicism, whose salad days came after 1800, suggests that the populace's appetite remained vital long after the critics' had been gorged. It has been argued that Gothicism remained a vogue in magazines until 1811 and perhaps later.[13]

Even after the noonday of Gothicism had become the evening of the genre, Gothicism continued as a creative force. John Polidori's *The Vampyre* (1819) opens a new vein of Gothic material that did not find its culmination until Bram Stoker's *Dracula* (1897). Mary Shelley's *Frankenstein* (1818) carried on the intellectual and humanistic strain of the genre begun by her father Godwin—one which became melded into the larger patterns of the Victorian novel of purpose. Moreover, Gothicism is obviously a major part of the tradition shared by the English Romantic poets. Less recognized are the contributions made by the Gothic novel to the development of fiction. Before the Gothic mode's encouragement of fear and suspense, character types provided the principal material of stories, as we can see in Henry Fielding's *Tom Jones* and Laurence Sterne's *Tristram Shandy*. Gothicism required attention to the plot and dramatic scenes as means of creating and maintaining interest (especially since the characters in the Gothic novel fairly quickly became conventions of the genre, including the innovative characters of Radcliffe and Lewis).

This interest in the plot, especially in the Radcliffean manner of explaining mysteries, led inevitably to the mystery story, whose apotheosis came near the beginning of that genre, in Wilkie Collins' *The Woman in White* (1859–60) and *The Moonstone* (1868), though it continues as a popular form today. Interest in the unconscious level of human behavior and in the darker side of humanity's impulses was in abeyance during the great period of the Victorian novel, a vehicle of sanity and ordinariness, although it appears clearly in the work of the Brontë sisters and in the great, later novels of Charles Dickens. The second-rank Victorian novelists —writers like William Harrison Ainsworth and Edward Bulwer-Lytton—borrowed heavily from the Gothicists' interest in horror and the past. Gothicism had a strong impress on nineteenth-century French writers like Honoré de Balzac, Eugène Sue, and Charles Baudelaire, all of whom expressly acknowledged the effect of *Melmoth*. Gothicism has delivered its finest fruits in America, though two of America's early practitioners, Edgar Allan Poe and Nathaniel Hawthorne, were reacting more to private impulses than to socio-political-literary conditions. The agony of hopelessly oppressed people have found perhaps their most humane and subtle expression in novels set in the American South—in the works of William Faulkner that explore aristocracy and slavery in an ever fluid society, and in the criticism of chaotic Protestantism in the work of the firm Catholic Flannery O'Connor.

YEARY LIBRARY
LAREDO JR. COLLEGE
LAREDO, TEXAS

CHAPTER 2

The Early Novels

I Fatal Revenge; or, the Family of Montorio *(1807)*

MATURIN named his first novel *The Family of Montorio;* but, much to his irritation, his publisher imposed the more compelling title *Fatal Revenge,* by which the novel is generally known. Fully aware that the evangelical-minded Anglican church of Ireland would not smile on a clergyman's appealing for public favor as the author of a sensational novel, Maturin published the book under the pseudonym of Dennis Jasper Murphy and at his own expense. Though the book has much effective language, it came too late after the novels it imitated to enjoy success. Nine years later, there were still forty copies unsold.[1]

Fatal Revenge is the most starkly Gothic in the joint traditions of Radcliffe and Lewis of any of Maturin's novels; *Melmoth the Wanderer* offers greater variety of mood. Lewis' influence is responsible for the detailed descriptions of revolting physical actions, machinations of witches, and conventual tombs in which drugged women are placed. Radcliffe furnishes the stronger formal influence; the denouement of *Fatal Revenge* reveals that most of the revolting details and all of the seemingly supernatural occurrences have been charades. Moreover, the management of the plot and the characters, especially the "frame" story and the mysterious, ultimately explained motivations of the monkish antagonist, are taken directly from *The Italian,* Radcliffe's finest novel. But, while no one can overlook the imitative qualities of Maturin's two Gothic novels— indeed, the imitative qualities of all of Maturin's works—the degree of their permanent interest relies not on what they borrow but on what they contribute. Maturin's originality in *Fatal Revenge* stems indirectly but inevitably from his interest in the nature of religious experience.

In the novel's preface, Maturin traces *"the fear arising from objects of invisible terror. . . .* to a high and obvious source" (italics Maturin's). Maturin may in part be defending himself against the irritation of the reader when he learns that the seemingly supernatural events of the story can be rationally explained. But, more pertinently, he is defending the plausibility of his characters' susceptibility to supernatural suggestions. Since the particular supernatural suggestion that the novel deals with is the obligation of two sons to murder their own father, the preface is essential to the rhetorical foundation of the novel. For example, one of the sons reflects late in his unwilling journey toward parricide that it is impious to contend with a spirit (the monk Schemoli) who can predict events accurately and who knows family secrets.

One of Maturin's best recent critics believes that Maturin's preface is simply a definition of the Gothic romance,[2] but the preface connotes broader matters. In most traditional Gothic romances, the heroes and heroines react straitlacedly in conventionally approved ways to unconventional situations. Horror arises from external threats, and little is learned about the characters' motivations—no more about the gentle Emily of *Udolpho* than about Lewis' Don Raymond or Lorenzo. In Maturin, on the other hand, the major characters react individually to unconventional situations. While the novel as a story remains absurd, the treatment of personality has elements of permanent interest.

Without being able to draw upon clinical psychology for confirmation of his insights, Maturin nevertheless attempts to define certain personality types susceptible to religious promptings capable of being perverted into areligious activity. Ippolito and Annibal, the brothers, are quite different psychological types: Ippolito customarily acts from impulse; Annibal, from conviction. They are in similar conditions, but Annibal is in the more critical and dangerous frame of mind. Impulse is more variable than conviction; Ippolito, therefore, has a built-in protection (his great agitations) from the horror of the deed he is made to contemplate: "Ippolito's emotions were vehement, [but] his mind was more disengaged than his brother's."

As an illustration of the classic form of the Radcliffean plot, it might be helpful to sketch the actions of the story. To do so distorts the effect of the novel even more than most summaries do. *Fatal Revenge* has such a complicated plot that Edith Birkhead says that many of the novel's readers "wander, bewildered, baffled, and distracted through labyrinthe mazes."[3] Although some of the hidden facts are revealed by obvious hints, the entire outline of events is made clear only by a long confessional letter late in the third volume, written by the monk Schemoli while under sentence of death. He has ingeniously plotted the death of his brother, the Count of Montorio. The following four paragraphs give the gist of that letter.

Schemoli's real name is Orazio Montorio, and as the elder brother he had held the title of count until his reported death some twenty years before the time of the novel's action. While a count, Orazio had married a reluctant Erminia di Amaldi. She was already secretly married to a cavalier, Verdoni; but she believed he had been killed by banditti and obeyed her worldly father's command to remain quiet about her child and to marry the wealthy Count Orazio. Shortly after the marriage, Verdoni, who had been held captive by the bandits, escaped and returned to find his wife remarried and the mother of Orazio's two sons. Deeply saddened, he planned to leave Italy forever; and Erminia, once she discovered Verdoni was still alive, intended to enter a convent after the birth of the child she was carrying.

In the meantime, though, she confessed her situation to Orazio's brother, an unfortunate choice for a confidant; for he was jealous of his brother's wealth and title, he had been a spurned lover of Erminia before she married Orazio, and he had an ambitious wife, Zenobia. (The scenes between Montorio and Zenobia are built upon the *Macbeth* motif of a vacillating husband and a ruthless wife.) The brother cleverly led Orazio to believe that his wife was unfaithful to him, a falsehood made easier to impart because Orazio had already felt that Erminia's lack of physical ardor meant that she did not love him. When Orazio saw Verdoni caressing a child that he was told was Erminia's his impulsive and vindictive nature drove him to prompt and mad action. He dragged Verdoni along a secret passageway to his wife's chambers in the Castle of Muralto. Refusing to listen to an explanation from Erminia, he had Verdoni stabbed slowly to death before her eyes. Upon Verdoni's death, Erminia's "heart burst," and she too died.

Orazio dashed away, indifferent to his worldly condition, and took up residence on an abandoned island near Greece, where he lived "a strange kind of animal life." A murderer in his brother's employ pursued him there, but Orazio anticipated the assault on his life and destroyed the assassin. Orazio read letters to the murderer from the present Count Montorio which proved Erminia's and Verdoni's innocence and his own brother's culpability; and he also learned through the letters that his two sons were dead. He decided that fit revenge would be to have Montorio die, and, to be certain that Montorio's descendants will not benefit by his infamy, he must be killed by his own sons.

Upon thinking of this scheme, typical of unspeakable Gothic villainy, Orazio ceased to be mad and wandered in Asia Minor fifteen years, learning occult secrets and increasing his physical powers. He eventually assumed the garb of a monk. Having decided that superstition was his only aid, he studied the "human character in its fiercer and gloomier features," in order to see how superstition, by exercise of art and terror, might best impel the passions to extremes. Prepared then to wreak his terrible vengeance, he became confessor to the Montorio family, keeping his face hidden with his cowl. At this point in time, the novel proper opens in the first volume, with Orazio's machinations against the sons of the fraudulent Count Montorio.

The two sons, Annibal and Ippolito, are both interested in "dark pursuits" and in manifestations of the supernatural, and both are courageous in facing the physical danger into which their curiosity leads them. But the brothers differ sharply in their attitudes toward life and the nature of experience. Ippolito, the elder, has excellent qualities but is a libertine; he is a lover of heroic adventure and a credulous lover of the "marvellous"—the striking and brilliant effects that give to the senses evidence of supernatural forces at work in the immediate world. Since Orazio has acutely diagnosed each of his nephews to know how to persuade them to believe that their murder of their father is an inevitable act willed by spiritual forces, to attract Ippolito he manipulates disappearances and appearances, and he hires a covey of "witches" who perform rites in a vault below the streets of a bustling Naples. The younger brother, Annibal, is a moody and distrustful youth who Orazio-Schemoli believes would at once see through the fantastical contrivings he employs against Ippolito, but who would be susceptible to suggestion. With Annibal, then, Schemoli uses less sensational, more curiosity-provoking situations to make him believe that uneasy spirits still move on the earth. The story of Annibal's seduction to

murder involves hidden staircases, a skeleton in a chest, a tomb
(Orazio's) without a corpse, and a servant afraid to reveal to Annibal certain secrets of the house of Montorio.

The first three-quarters of the novel is taken up with the brothers' separate courses to parricide, and the reader is unaware of
Schemoli's motivations. Ippolito lives in Naples; Annibal, with
their parents at the Castle of Muralto; and they do not meet in the
novel until shortly before they kill their father. Their tales are
given in alternating chapters, initially in letters written by the
brothers to each other, then by omniscient narration. The more
complicated course, Ippolito's, is initiated by mysterious ques-
tions and commands of a stranger while Ippolito is getting out of
cabs or while he is enjoying his dissipations, and by letters left in
his rooms. (Ippolito does not know the stranger is his father's confessor Schemoli.) A conflict is set up between this stranger and a
youth named Cyprian, who becomes Ippolito's servant and who
attempts to keep Ippolito from his scenes of former dissipation
by using "*female blandishments*" (italics are Maturin's). (The end
of the novel reveals that Cyprian is a nun who fell in love with
Ippolito by sight and left her convent in order to live near him.
She eventually dies of the effects of suppressing her passion.)

Cyprian's influence, however, is ineffective; Ippolito shortly
begins to have midnight assignations with the stranger. Having
prepared Ippolito by telling him that he is doomed to commit a
horrible crime, the stranger takes him to a subterranean chamber
where his fate will supposedly be revealed to him after he has killed
a strapped-down figure. Driven by the temptation that he will
thereby be raised out of the ordinary nature of humanity, Ippolito
"almost without consciousness" stabs the victim, who, when uncovered, resembles Ippolito's father, but is in fact only an ingeniously constructed dummy. Believing he has actually killed
someone, and in horror at the evident thought that this murder
somehow spiritually presages the death of his father, Ippolito flees
Naples and wanders in the countryside. His reputation for dealing
with shameful mysteries has preceded him, and he finds it difficult
to locate lodgings and impossible to escape his thoughts.

When the stranger appears suddenly one day and asks, "Why
do you linger here?" Ippolito pursues him and eventually descends
a deep, winding staircase to one of the most elaborate systems of

underground passageways in Gothic fiction. After stumbling on rags and human bones, he sees the stranger coming up to him through the "thick vapours of the vault." The stranger says that Ippolito will do the deed that he must do in three months. The stranger then moves off with his customary, incredible speed, and Ippolito follows in search of him through immensely long corridors. He eventually spies him and a monk carrying a figure in white; the stranger leaves, and the monk prepares to stab the figure in white. Ippolito frightens him off and takes the figure, an unconscious female, into the open air of a convent garden where she revives. He discovers that she is in love with his brother Annibal. Preparing to flee by boat with her, he is borne off by the river suddenly agitated by an earthquake, leaving her on the bank and presuming her to be killed by the turbulence. Ippolito is then arrested by the Inquisition. Another earthquake frees Ippolito from the prison, and he attempts to flee on a boat bound to Sicily; but, as the stranger had predicted, the ocean, in the form of a volcanic eruption that destroys the ship, throws him back on the shore. Only Ippolito of all those on the boat survives, and once on the shore he finds the stranger waiting for him. Worn down by strain and superstitious apprehension, Ippolito thereupon surrenders his will to the stranger.

All the while that Ippolito has been drawing out Schemoli's theatricalness and the accidents of nature, Annibal has been prying into the secrets of the Castle of Muralto. Annibal has learned that an old family servant, Michelo, knows some family secrets; and, when the servant tells him that he had been in the former Count's dark tomb and had felt a cold bony hand touch his face, Annibal eagerly decides to explore the matter. He first examines the shut-up apartments that had served as the bridal suite of Orazio, which the present Count had ordered closed forever. (A set of closed apartments, where a dark deed has occurred or where ghosts walk, is a standard setting in a Gothic novel.) On the first visit, Annibal falls in love with a portrait of the Countess Erminia, whom he feels is still alive.

On a second visit, Annibal hears a ghostly voice and sees an eye in a tapestry appear to look from side to side and finally to glare at a particular spot on a wall (a standard Radcliffean device). Struck with amazement and fear, Annibal tears off part of the wainscoting and descends a passage the wall had blocked off. He finds a plastered-over door; and, within a chamber behind the door, he finds a chest containing a skeleton, whose hand had been severed from the arm. He thinks it might be Count Orazio, killed on "that terrible night" that Michelo has vaguely alluded to. (The skeleton is actually that of Verdoni, of course.) Annibal thereupon decides to watch the tomb of Orazio, for there human agents may be at work, and they are less fearful than the evidently genuine ghost of the tapestry (who is, naturally, Schemoli, standing behind the tapestry and looking out through holes he had cut). What happens at the tomb, however, is that Michelo disappears when Annibal leaves him briefly to pursue a pale, large figure; and, when they meet again, Michelo is in a "prophetic ecstasy," speaking of "woe" and of the necessity that the house of Montorio fall. He claims he is being controlled by someone not alive; the being had lain in Count Orazio's coffin, but what he said to Michelo is lost because Michelo dies just as he is about to relate this most crucial point.

Filippo, Michelo's nephew, tells Annibal of figures, one in monk's habit, that he has seen down a "secret" corridor, and the two decide to search the castle. They discover that the skeleton is no longer in the closed-off apartments, and Annibal is apprehended by the present Count Montorio and Schemoli, who lock him in a dusty room for several days, where a gloomy Schemoli visits him once a day. Ultimately, Schemoli concocts the confession that his was the skeleton Annibal had found, that his spirit has been imprisoned in the body of a man dead for two thousand years, and that he is forced to live on, conscious of the ways of the dead, until his murderer is killed. Annibal is proud of talking with spirits; and, Faust-like, he swears allegiance to Schemoli if Schemoli will tell him secrets of the dead. He nonetheless shrinks from Schemoli's revelation that he, Annibal, is the one chosen to avenge his, Schemoli's, murder; and that the one he must kill is his own father, whose guilty demeanor he had long suspected.

Dismayed by the results of his curiosity, and longing for normal happiness, Annibal escapes from Muralto with the aid of Filippo and goes to the countryside seeking peace and quiet. A religious procession with relics attracts him, and he sees a novitiate who resembles the portrait of the Countess Erminia. He saves her life when an earthquake causes a river to flood and learns that her name is Ildefonsa (supposedly of illegitimate birth, she is actually the daughter of Erminia and Verdoni, a fact not given until Schemoli's confession). The two communicate through notes dropped in flowers, and Ildefonsa eventually agrees to trust herself to his sense of honor and to flee with him at the first opportunity. Schemoli appears on the scene in the role of Catholic persecutor of reluctant novitiates, and he gives to Ildefonsa a drug that causes a deathlike state. At this point, Ippolito saves Ildefonsa from the monk's dagger and is separated from her by the agitation of the river. When Annibal and Ildefonsa are reunited, they reside with Filippo in the forest for some time. Trying to reach Puzzoli and safety, they are misled by their guide and waylaid. Filippo is killed, and Annibal and Ildefonsa taken captive and separated. Schemoli's prediction is fulfilled: the object of Annibal's love had been taken from him "at the moment of possession, and life had changed its complexion at the moment it was becoming bright with hope and joy." Like Ippolito only two days before, Annibal gives his will to Schemoli.

They go separately to Muralto, where Annibal finds Ildefonsa dying of poison administered by the countess, whose jealousy of Erminia had been reawakened by her husband's dressing Erminia's daughter in elaborate gowns in memory of his early love. On the night planned for the murder of the Count, the conscience-and-fear-wracked Count Montorio confesses to Schemoli that he had kept one fact from him. To make a partial reparation to his betrayed sister-in-law and his brother, he had taken their two sons and reared them as his own to inherit the title at his death, and he had propagated the false rumor that Orazio's sons had died. The agonized Schemoli tries to halt the brothers on their way to Montorio's chambers; but, stupefied, they do not notice his speechless contortions, and they walk by him to their "inevitable doom." Their "swords met in their father's body."

Deeply contrite, Schemoli confesses his deed and writes the account of his life given at the opening of this plot summary. He dies of a broken blood vessel just before his scheduled execution. His dying exultation is that "The last of the Montorios has not perished on a scaffold"—a vainglorious assertion of Gothic pride in noble villainy already used by Schedoni in Radcliffe's *The Italian* and used again by Maturin in *Bertram*. The brothers, broken in spirit and exiled, become army officers and successfully seek death at the siege of Barcelona in 1697.

As difficult as it may be to follow the paraphrase above, the entire plot of *Fatal Revenge* is vastly more complex and colorful than any summation could suggest. Not only does my paraphrase give in chronological order what the novel presents through a series of flashbacks, but there are several digressive stories, the most successful of which is the suspense-filled account of Filippo's escape from an assassin hired by the fraudulent Count Montorio, who is afraid that Filippo may know too much about the skeleton in the passageway. The pace and organization of this story lead us to suspect that Maturin's best genre may be the vignette, not the novel—a suspicion confirmed by the multiple stories that make up *Melmoth the Wanderer*.

In addition to illustrating the nature of a Gothic story, the paraphrase suggests other features of Gothic esthetics; most relevant are Schemoli's activities. He always moves with fantastic speed (Ippolito on a galloping horse cannot keep sight of him), and he enters the prison of the Inquisition to visit Ippolito in his cell. As his confession makes clear, he has no truly supernatural powers, only great physical endurance and the tricks he learned in Asia Minor—not to mention cleverness. But Maturin does not permit human limitations to restrict Schemoli's activities significantly. The necessity to keep the two temptations going simultaneously, often at a fever pitch, has Orazio dashing from Ildefonsa's convent to the areas of Ippolito's wandering, back to the convent to prepare for Ildefonsa's opiate-induced "death," and from there to entice Ippolito to enter the subterranean passageway, and finally, back again to the convent's underground cemetery to arrange for Ildefonsa's murder.

In the earlier part of the book, the simultaneous temptations of Annibal and Ippolito are somewhat more acceptable; but even here Orazio's efficiency precludes total plausibility. He is, at the same general span of time, accustomed each night to visit (1) Ippolito in Naples, (2) the imprisoned Annibal in Muralto, and (3) the tomb of Erminia, where he penitentially bleeds himself; and he also often visits at night the closed-off apartments that he had once shared with Erminia. Finally, there is no adequate explanation of how Schemoli managed to be at the precise point of the shoreline where

Ippolito washed ashore after the eruption of an undersea volcano had destroyed the boat he was on.

Ernest Baker says that Orazio "embodies traits of the Wandering Jew from Godwin's *St. Leon* and Lewis' *Monk*";[4] but, more essentially, Orazio conforms to the Radcliffean concept of a mere human villain whose supernatural appearance is deceptive. The inconsistencies and the incredible simultaneous actions, though they are more grossly employed in *Fatal Revenge* than is customary, are a natural result of the Gothicists' obsession with the immediate effect of a scene or atmosphere. The idea that readers might want a clear time scheme and plausible relationships among actions seldom occurred to Gothic novelists.

The love affairs in the novel also follow Gothic precedents in their basic conceptions. Cyprian, as a nun who flees her convent for love, comes from *The Monk;* and Ildefonsa's treatment as a novice at the hands of Schemoli and her Abbess is not only standard Gothic fare but anticipates Maturin's subsequently more virulent portrayals of the unnaturalness of conventual life. Annibal's falling in love with his half-sister is a tired bit of Gothicism that Maturin does not know what to do with; by the time Annibal learns of his relationship, he is more depressed by the thought of his guilt for murder than by the "horrors of *incest.*"

As I have said, *Fatal Revenge* is a Radcliffean romance in that all of the seeming supernaturalness is explained in a rush toward the end of the novel by Schemoli's confessional letter. But there is one feature to the ending of *Fatal Revenge* that is unlike that of Radcliffe's *Mysteries of Udolpho* or *The Italian.* In *Udolpho,* the revelations toward the end of the novel of the real causes of mysterious circumstances have no effect upon the basic structural balance of the novel. Emily has throughout the novel been the main object of attention; she remains such during the revelations, which are fairly brief. In *The Italian,* Schedoni and Vivaldi had shared the primary interest, and both are actors in the scenes of revelation. In *Fatal Revenge,* on the other hand, the revelations cause a total *volte-face* of reader concern. Until the last quarter of the last volume, the main interest has been in the two brothers and in the self-delusive and perverse manner in which they individually allow themselves to be psychologically coerced into committing one of

the greatest of social crimes. The progress of each may be redundant
of the other's—for example, each regrets his thoughtless early
interest in supernaturalism, each surrenders to Schemoli when a
prediction comes true, each is helped or hindered by earthquakes
miraculously local in effect; and Maturin may be obtrusive in mark-
ing out for the reader each of the several stages in the brothers'
progress. But, during the individual stages, Maturin traces with
insight and expository skill the feelings of the brothers as they
attempt to learn whether they can escape from Schemoli's pre-
dictions that they will of necessity kill their own father. With the
advent of the Radcliffean confession of Schemoli, the structure that
has held together organically for some twelve hundred and fifty
pages is thrust aside.

This violation of structural consistency has some potential for
meaningful variety, but unfortunately such variety is not forth-
coming. Orazio is a powerfully passionate figure, and he is an
energetic schemer against the brothers; but as a repentant, mag-
nificently suffering jealous husband and murderer, he is dull, prolix,
and self-consciously posturing. By the time he reveals himself,
we have already seen the complexity of the brothers' developing
feelings; and, in comparison to those, Orazio's agonizings seem
sudden and insufficiently prepared for. His erratic behavior and
rumored cruelty when he had been Count are never explained;
neither motivation nor natural malice is adduced to support his
actions—only that he is "Italian." Later, in carrying out his scheme
for revenge, he simply does what the occasion calls for in order to
make the action more sensational. Like Ippolito, he is impulsive;
but he never reflects in the least, whereas Ippolito withholds himself from any immediate commitment to the idea that he must do
murder. Orazio's short-lived inner moral tensions have not the
nearest degree of interest to those of the brothers, whose inclinations to the darker sides of experience are leavened by manliness,
morality, and integrity. Part of the cause of the slackness of Orazio's
characterization probably derives from Maturin's assumption that
lovers of Gothicism would transfer to Orazio-Schemoli the fully
motivated attributes of Ann Radcliffe's Schedoni. And, indeed,
reading in sequence *The Italian* and *Fatal Revenge* makes Schemoli
more impressive; but reading Radcliffe is no way to evaluate the
skill of Maturin.

Most critics of Maturin have not evaluated *Fatal Revenge* as I have; indeed, some have found Schemoli's confession the most engrossing part of the entire three volumes.[5] Their preference is based on the force and vigor of Orazio's language, which Walter Scott illustrates with the following passage describing Orazio's state of mind during his flight following Erminia's death:

> My reason was not suspended, it was totally *changed*. I had become a kind of intellectual savage; a being, that with the malignity and depravation of inferior natures, still retains the reason of a man, and retains it only for his curse. Oh! that midnight darkness of the soul, in which it seeks for something whose loss has carried away every sense but one of utter and desolate privation; in which it traverses leagues in motion and worlds in thought, without consciousness of relief, yet with a dread of pausing. I had nothing to seek, nothing to recover; the whole world could not restore me an atom, could not shew me again a glimpse of what I had been or lost; yet I rushed on as if the next step would reach shelter and peace.

Another point concerning Orazio's story is made by Idman: "The progress of the violent action is admirably concentrated, and the rapidity and poignancy of the style is powerfully indicative of the anguish felt by the writer." But these are not qualities of Orazio's story alone. As I say above, Maturin writes well in short bursts, and Orazio's story is only one hundred and thirty-two pages long in the large-print, generously margined first edition. Other short sections, such as Ippolito pursuing Schemoli and saving Ildefonsa in the subterranean chapters, are equally "concentrated" and are even more relevant to Maturin's basic interest, the spirit of religion. The kind of passage admired by Scott is not found only in the concluding confession; for Ippolito, Annibal, even Montorio and Zenobia speak in comparably intense language, though perhaps not with the energy of Orazio in his despair. (One suspects, especially in light of *Melmoth the Wanderer,* that Maturin identifies more with the characters with the bleaker souls than with the comparatively more innocent characters. This self-identification may help to explain Maturin's neglecting to delineate Orazio's motivations more objectively.)

Maturin's language, while verbose and somewhat derivative in imagery, has an impetus and imaginative life. Indeed, it is ironic that the basic structural lesion in the novel develops partially from the effectiveness of the language. The linguistic quality of

Ippolito's and Annibal's mental plights creates strong interest in the two young men, while a contradictory sympathy—for the cause of the brothers' miseries—is created by the novel's concluding emphasis upon Orazio-Schemoli. The disparate natures of the two sections—the finely traced motivations of Ippolito and Annibal, and the straightforward destructiveness of Orazio-Schemoli— are not absorbed into a uniform esthetic experience.

Despite the ill effect of the abrupt change in the center of interest, Maturin took considerable pains in planning the novel. With the possible exception of the laboriously historical *The Albigenses,* no other Maturin novel was so carefully contrived before its writing. The alternation of the early chapters between Annibal and Ippolito, though blatant and rather ridiculous in that Ippolito keeps scoffing Annibal's childishness when *he* has *serious* ghosts to contend with, provides a good example of Maturin's consciously structuring the novel. At the end of the first volume he quite skillfully pulls the two skeins together so that they begin to run simultaneously. Also, Maturin's delaying the appearance of Count Montorio and the monk Schemoli (in his "own" person) until after there have been three hundred and twenty pages of hints about their centrality to Annibal's and Ippolito's problems increases the suspense both about them and about the activities of Montorio's "sons." *Fatal Revenge,* like most Gothic novels that were written in imitation of Radcliffe, has many inconsistencies and several weakly explained mysteries; and there are innumerable indications within the text that the novel is an unrevised first draft. But despite all its flaws, bombast, and excessive sentimentality, it is an impressive first novel.

II   The Wild Irish Boy *(1808)*

Maturin struck the nadir in his practice of fiction early in his career. Not enough biographical data remains for this period in Maturin's life for us to conjecture confidently the cause of the careless writing that is to blame for most of the false starts, digressions, changes in technique, redundancies, and grossness of characterization that are found in *The Wild Irish Boy.* One of the digressions in the novel, on the pernicious effect of making a cleric supplement his income by tutoring, suggests that his second profession of teaching was pressing upon his attention. It is not known for certain, though, whether Maturin took in students before his father's ruin made it imperative that he do so;[6] so this digression may be, in hindsight, only ironic.

The progression of events in *The Wild Irish Boy* is, quite obviously, improvised as the pen moves. The method of narration shifts constantly, frequently without even such devices as a "white space" or a new chapter to indicate that a change might be expected. The novel begins as an epistolary tale, the greater part of the material coming from the pen of Elmaide St. Clair, describing her desperate love for Ormsby Bethel. Suddenly the narration shifts to the first person, and Elmaide is heard from again only once—which is not surprising, since the first-person narrator is Ormsby, and he does not even learn Elmaide's name until a few pages from the end of the novel, by which time she has died. To increase the mystery of the narrator's stance, the first four hundred pages of Ormsby's narration is his autobiography, itself contained in a letter; and the change from letter-autobiography to orthodox first person is so indistinct as to be easily overlooked. At times during both kinds of narration the narrator assumes a breadth of experience and tone of wisdom inappropriate for the mercurial eighteen-year-old hero, in order to lecture on such topics as Dublin College and the shallowness of Irishmen. Nor is confusion with the narrative perspective the story's only liability. The novel is loaded with digressions and flashbacks, as Maturin attempts to build enough verbiage to fill out the three volumes.

This and his next novel, *The Milesian Chief,* constitute Maturin's major effort to draw upon his native land's traditions as material, an effort most likely inspired in equal degree by his love of Ireland and by his hope to benefit from the interest in Irish matters engendered by the Act of Union (January 1, 1801) and by Maria Edgeworth's novels. Maturin draws most heavily upon the legendary Milesians, who were reputedly the traditional rulers of Ireland and were descendants of Milesius, a Phoenician trader who settled Hibernia and brought it the culture of the East and Greece. The Milesian chiefs demanded and received total obeisance from their native Irish followers. As Ireland came progressively under English control, many of the chiefs remained by treaty free from any personal restraint by English law. The Act of Union and the hostilities with England in 1798 ruined most of the chiefs whose property had not already been sequestered during the Puritan Wars to be given to Oliver Cromwell's supporters; but some of them continued to live in poverty in their ancestral mansions and castles.

The plot of this novel is complicated, but the writing is considerably less inventive than that of *Fatal Revenge*. The hero Ormsby is the illegitimate son of Miss Percival, who pretends that Ormsby's father is Mr. Bethel, whom she is presently serving as governess for their unacknowledged daughter, Sybilla. Ormsby's uncle DeLacy, one of Ireland's few remaining rich Milesians, prefers Ormsby for his heir, despite his illegitimacy, because he is in the male line of descent, while the other aspirant, Captain Deloraine, is DeLacy's sister's son. While their uncle lives, Deloraine attempts to cause Ormsby to violate the old man's principles and thus lose his favor. He nearly succeeds, particularly since Ormsby is very simple and trusting; but, by fighting Lord Roschamp to prevent his mother from eloping with a servant after Mr. Bethel's death, Ormsby solidly gains the proud Milesian's approval. Then, acting on the advice of a mysterious figure who lives in a solitary tower, Ormsby saves his uncle from being strangled by an assassin, who escapes.

Meanwhile, Ormsby has fallen in love with Lady Montrevor, the unloved and unloving wife of an English nobleman living in temporary exile in Ireland. Although Lady Montrevor tells Ormsby she thinks of him only as a grandson or a son, Ormsby remains infatuated with the beautiful woman of the world, who drops her pretense of vanity before Ormsby's sincere adoration to reveal that she despises in her soul the social acclaim she seeks. Ormsby's uncle discovers from Ormsby that the cause of his despondency is to be found at Montrevor-House. Misunderstanding, DeLacy courts Lady Montrevor's daughter, Athanasia, for Ormsby and then tells him to come to claim the prize, having had the forethought to have a bishop at hand to marry them. Ormsby begins to love his wife out of melancholy and pity, but he remains interested primarily in Lady Montrevor.

When Ormsby becomes independently situated with £5000 a year upon the death of his uncle, he goes to London with his wife and her family. While Deloraine serves as his estate manager back in Ireland, Ormsby is taken up by the social whirl in London. He remains faithful to his wife, despite some determined and protracted wooing by Lady Delphina Orberry. To force Ormsby to surrender to her, Lady Orberry encourages him in gambling, at which he beggars himself; but his virtue remains unassailable.

Lord Montrevor accuses Ormsby of being Lady Montrevor's lover; and Lady Montrevor's eldest daughter, the wife of a powerful political figure, runs off with one of her husband's discharged employees after it is learned that she has been running a crooked gambling casino in her townhouse. Lord Montrevor dies in a duel with the ex-employee; Lady Orberry poisons herself for sexual frustration; and the virtuous survivors eventually return to Ireland. Deloraine, who had been deliberately mismanaging Ormsby's Irish properties and attempting to seduce Athanasia, shoots himself for fear of discovery. The denouement has Ormsby realize his wife's virtues, and Lady Montrevor marries the man who earlier in the novel had lived in the solitary tower. This man turns out to be not only her first love, whom she had disaffected in their youth by a disdainful act of pride, but Ormsby's real father and the brother of Mr. Bethel. After briefly giving way to dissipation because of the alienation of his true affections, he had dropped Miss Percival shortly before his brother had taken her as his mistress. He had not been aware of his paternity until Miss Percival had confessed to him shortly before she died.

The climactic series of events, sketched in the preceding paragraph, is hard to unravel because the chaos of Ormsby's life is communicated in part by the disorder of the narration of the last part of the novel. Indeed, Maturin's plot becomes so gnarled that he turns the tower-dweller into a *deus ex machina* to resolve it. Learning he is Ormsby's father, he confounds Deloraine's plot to bankrupt Ormsby and goes to London to extricate his son from Lady Orberry's increasing entrapment.

The ludicrous and erratic plot does not cause the novel's failure so much as do the characters, who are either eccentric exotics or cardboard cutouts. Lady Montrevor, the most satisfactory creation, is among the eccentrics; but her unhumorous wit and stiff lectures on interior decoration (obviously Maturin's early concept of aristocratic conversation) do not diminish her thematic comments on the necessity to live one's inner life on principle whatever face one must present to the world. To an extent, in fact, Maturin succeeds with Lady Montrevor in presenting a complex figure. The sensual ladies Orberry, Castle-Wycomb, and Westhampton (the

latter two are Lady Montrevor's daughters) are evidently intended
to portray the corruption of English high society during the contemporary Napoleonic struggles. But their presentation is totally
superficial, and Lady Orberry's dissolution into a suicide after
being such a vicious schemer is particularly so melodramatic that
the reader sees the three women as simply harlots and their creator
a panderer to licentious interest. Miss Percival, who has some
substance as a characterization because of her efforts to intellectual-
ly justify her immorality, plays only a small role; and her repeated
readiness to rob her children and run off with any available man
turns her, too, into a caricature that is heightened by her ultimate
repentance and death.

Ormsby postures throughout, throwing himself on his knees
before one female after the other, pleading either for affection or
for mercy; his manliness in defending Miss Percival and in saving
his uncle's life is not illustrated again. His frequent recourse to
gambling is not a modification of his role as sentimental hero so
much as it is an intensification of it. The sentimental hero is tradi-
tionally tempted, and few other sentimental heroes are as subject
to such extremes of passive, will-less dissipation and flamboyantly
rhetorical recognition of virtue, so contiguous as to be nearly simultaneous. Unremarkably, these exaggerations of mood make Ormsby
duller rather than more complex.

The Wild Irish Boy is not a Gothic novel, although the language
—especially during the extravagance of Ormsby's reactions—
approximates Gothic rhetoric. For example, Ormsby "foamed with
fury" while he threatened "instant death" to the servant upon
finding him with his mother in Lord Roschamp's house. In being
warned by the stranger to save his uncle from murder, Ormsby
feels the "melancholy shade" of his mind deepening "almost into
terror," and his description of being nearly fatally strangled himself by his uncle's assailant has something of the obsession with
aberrant states of mind that provides the originality of Maturin's
greater novels:

I did not lose my faculties: I did not lose my horror of the death; I felt
all its bitterness—the suppression of my breath, the labouring and con-
vulsions of my chest, the bloody flashes that seemed to dart from my eyes,
and lastly, every object of the night swimming before me, and every one

with blood-streaked and glaring eyes that stared on me; and my tormentor changed into a fiend, whose bulk was like that of a mountain, whose talons were tipped with burning iron, and whose mouth and eyes breathed flames into mine—it was an horrible agony.

Some descriptions of Lady Montrevor's seeing her lover from her youth also partake of the fear of the dead that the Gothic reeks of: and, of course, Ormsby's love for his mother-in-law and eventual stepmother is a play upon the Gothic motif of incest.

But, by and large, Maturin is on a new tack in this novel. Searching after the failure of *Fatal Revenge* for a popular vein he could profitably tap, Maturin wrote what might best be termed a society romance. Maturin also relied upon the salability of scandal, especially in the last volume's depiction of the promiscuity and corruption of Lady Montrevor's married daughters and of the social class to which they belong. That there are no actual presentations of the sex act does not make this volume the less surprising production of a clergyman who at this time believed that his major ambition, and his best chance in life, was to achieve preferment in the Church. (The appeal of sex in *The Wild Irish Boy* is more as prurience than as moral *exempla*.) In any case, judging from the flowery descriptions of the ball-room scenes and the artificiality of the aristocratic and "witty" conversations, Maturin was not writing from personal acquaintance of the social class he was libeling.

The title of the novel is an obvious borrowing from Sydney Owenson (later Lady Morgan), who in 1806 had published *The Wild Irish Girl*. Lady Montrevor once appears at a ball dressed as Glorvina, the Wild Irish Girl, daughter of a Milesian chieftain, thereby making clear Maturin's attempt to benefit from Miss Owenson's great success. The attempt may have been a last-minute one, for there are only few parallels between the novels. Maturin's novel is neither pro-Irish nor anti-Irish; unlike *The Milesian Chief*, depictions of Irish life are not concrete, with the exception of a brief description of the improvident hangers-on and retainers at DeLacy's castle. The novel's only review irritatedly points out that Maturin's hero is not even Irish, "but is born in France, and educated in England; his mother is an English woman."[7] Niilo Idman accepts only the Milesian as deriving from Owenson's tale.[8] That Maturin could borrow more extensively, and to somewhat better purpose, is proved by his next novel.

III   The Milesian Chief *(1811)*

In *The Milesian Chief* Maturin delivered what his second novel, by allusion in its title to *The Wild Irish Girl,* had indirectly promised: a study of Irish national life. The study is vitiated by the posturing and lurid speeches of the major character, but it is superior in some respects to Owenson's story, which is composed largely of historical accounts and of folkloristic anecdotes about Irish bards and heroes in the text and in scholarly footnotes. Owenson is interested almost solely in tracing contemporary remnants of Milesian influence, which Maturin scarcely touches upon, probably with the assumption that the wide circulation of *The Wild Irish Girl* made explanations on his part superfluous. Owenson utilized her antiquarian interests to demonstrate the dignity of the Irish nation; and the novel's popularity stemmed largely from this aspect.[9] Maturin did not try to add anything to Owenson's researches about life in Connaught, the western part of Ireland that is the stronghold of Milesian legend and descendants.

Owenson's book is itself an effort to exploit a growing interest in both Ireland and England about the "relics of the ancient order as had managed to survive"[10] centuries of war and especially the efforts of the English to obliterate reminders that the Irish were once ruled by their own hereditary princes and counseled by a Catholic church that had spawned innumerable monasteries. Charlotte Brooke's *Reliques of Irish Poetry* (1789), the *Anthologia Hibernica* (1793–94), and Edward Bunting's *The Ancient Music of Ireland* (1796) helped to establish the curiosity that Owenson fed. Thomas Moore's *Irish Melodies* followed her novel by two years, in 1808; but his work was widely known in manuscript before her novel was published.

Maturin's borrowings from Owenson's book are obvious in *The Milesian Chief.* Each novel has an Irish chief with a pedigree that extends to pre-Christian times who loses his wealth to an Englishman; and each chief sees a member of his family fall in love with someone in the usurper's family. The books also differ, of course. The Milesian chief in *The Wild Irish Girl* is innately noble, refusing to ask guests to leave even though his entertainment of them is speeding his bankruptcy; the chieftain in *The Milesian Chief* is irascible and finally goes insane. He is thereby incapacitated as a dominant character, and the major Milesian character in Maturin's novel is not the chieftain but his grandsón. *The Wild Irish Girl* ends happily with the marriage of Glorvina and the son; the father intends to alleviate the lot of his Irish dependents and to educate the English into considering the Irish as a responsible, hard-working people. *The Milesian Chief* ends in unhappiness for the characters, and presumably the English oppression of the Irish will continue.

Both authors are sympathetic to the Irish poor and to the Irish nation, controlled by an English people whose governors and viceroys pride themselves on their ignorance of, and their contempt for, the affairs of the people they rule. Maturin is as familiar as Owenson with the sordidness of the life of the Irish peasant; but Owenson offers commonplace detail, while Maturin emphasizes the grotesque and vivid. A description of an Irish peasant's hut illustrates Owenson's technique. The door of the hut, loose from its hinges, serves when propped up as a barrier to keep a child inside as in an animal pen. The hut has only two rooms. One, for human and animal sleeping, contains only straw; the other, for the human beings' activities, contains a single stool, which at meals holds the smoking hot potatoes which are the family's sole food. The description is neither sentimental nor overdrawn, but presented as an incidental observation during a walk. Both Maturin and Owenson offer skillful descriptions of stormy land- and seascapes in western Ireland.

Maturin's forte, and Owenson's weakness, is in the presentation of passion. Though Owenson's book is epistolary—letters from the pen of the younger son who becomes steadily more in love with Glorvina—the emotion is pallid and unruffled. A few scenes are realistically presented, such as the son's jealous anger when he suspects that Glorvina's affection for him is the residue of her feeling for her first lover; but an extreme pitch of emotion is constant in Maturin; and, while it is somewhat wearying, it is frequently effective. Owenson's novel has practically no narrative interest: Glorvina is loved by both the father and the son, but the reader does not know of the father's affection until the last few pages. As soon as the father learns of his son's infatuation, he puts aside his own interests to sponsor those of his son.

As in discussions of most of Maturin's works, a summary of the plot of *The Milesian Chief* helps to acquaint the reader with the relationships among events that need to be commented upon. The Milesian chieftain in this novel has lost his hereditary estates through bankruptcy to Lord Montclare, and he lives with his grandson Connal O'Morven in a ruined watchtower on the border of his former estate. Lord Montclare's sister had married the chieftain's son without consulting the wishes either of Lord Montclare or of the chieftain, neither of whom approved. Nevertheless, Lord Montclare acquiesced in his sister's deathbed plea that he take care of her family. He appointed her husband (the former heir to the estate) his land steward; and the younger son, Desmond O'Morven, accepted a commission in the army. The elder son Connal, who refused any help, is being secretly prepared by his grandfather to lead an uprising of the Irish masses loyal to the Milesian tradition.

Lord Montclare has for most of his life lived on the Continent in order to better cultivate the immense musical and intellectual talents of his daughter Armida. Mystery surrounds him: his mind is melancholy; he changes residence often; and he is tormented by a monk. (These motifs from the Gothic tale are used only incidentally in this novel.) When the monk, Morosini, begins to threaten him, he flees to England, where another of his nephews, Colonel Wandesford, is accepted as Armida's fiancé—eagerly by Montclare, reluctantly by Armida. Father and daughter then go to Ireland, where Colonel Wandesford will join them, because Montclare's contempt for the country's inhabitants inures him against the possible revelation of the secret that is the source of his melancholy. Nevertheless, terror at its imminent revelation puts him in his deathbed, where he has barely enough time to tell his secret to Armida before he dies.

His Italian wife had given birth only to daughters, of whom only the first, Armida, survived. Since Montclare had married in the first place solely in the hopes of having a son in order to keep the O'Morvens from inheriting their old estate through Randal O'Morven's marriage with his sister, he was driven to the desperate device of promoting the rumor that his wife has died so he could marry again. He was stunned by the news that in her retreat his wife has given birth to a son. Fearful of making public his nefarious lie about his wife's death, and wanting yet to frustrate the O'Morvens,

Montclare remained silent, suffering mental torture at the threats of Morosini.

But Lord Montclare himself did not have quite all of the facts. His son, Endymion, it turns out in good time, is not a son at all but a daughter who has been kept ignorant of her own sex so that Lady Montclare can have a defense against her husband's schemes as well as a claim on the estates when he dies. On crossing from England to Ireland as her mother pursues Lord Montclare, Endymion is saved from drowning by Desmond O'Morven, who feels an attraction for the young "man" that he tries to reject. There are several scenes of what seems to be a blatant homosexual affinity, which distinguishes Maturin's development upon Shakespeare's employments of sexual disguise; in Shakespeare, everyone knows at least his own sex even if he cannot be sure of anybody else's. The ludicrousness inherent in this aspect of the plot has a double apotheosis. Lady Montclare attempts to seduce Desmond so he will not reveal Endymion's sex, "in vain hoping to make the slave of her passions the confidant of her secret"; and Endymion, upon learning that she is a "woman," is terrified that she will be killed by Lady Montclare, even though she does not know yet what being a "woman" means. But the Endymion matter is largely a diversion from the main plot: it provides, although unnecessarily, an explanation of how the O'Morvens are being cheated of the rightful inheritance of their ancestral properties.

The main story deals with the powerful love that springs up immediately upon the meeting between Connal O'Morven and Armida. Both are stupendously, heroically proud—Connal, of his heritage and inevitably noble death; Armida, of the beauty and talents that have gained her applause in every city of the Continent. Armida, incensed when she sees Connal with a beautiful girl and her baby, becomes ill with restrained passion and curiosity. Finally the girl herself tells Armida that she did indeed love Connal but that the baby is Colonel Wandesford's and that Connal was merely trying to reconcile her to life and to restore her to virtuous paths. Connal admits his great love for Armida but pridefully declares that, because of their family quarrel, they cannot meet again. Armida nonetheless breaks her engagement to Wandesford, declaring that his own depravity has absolved her from fulfilling it.

Maturin, an opponent of the Act of Union of 1801, uses the

uprising of 1798 as a major part of the novel's backdrop, though loosely and with no effort to trace the actual events, most of which occurred in east Ireland. Wandesford stumbles across a meeting of Irishmen planning to rebel against the English. Connal has just convinced them that they cannot defeat the English nor could Ireland survive as an independent country; and he prevents the rebels from killing Wandesford when the officer promises not to reveal their aborted plans. Wandesford breaks his word, however; and the rebellion begins as self-defense. Armida initially plans to go to the besieged Irish, saying she is "overcome by passion and destiny." But on her way she comes across Connal walking at night with his arm about Lady Gabrielle, who has long loved him; and Armida returns to the castle and renews her engagement to Wandesford, who has been given orders to crush the rebellion.

Wandesford is captured by the rebels, but is again released by Connal, who thinks Wandesford is by this time Armida's husband. By a coincidence, Armida remains in Connal's custody long enough for him to learn the truth. In turn, she learns that Connal had been escorting Gabrielle home after she had come to him on her own initiative, wishing to become his mistress. After several passionate scenes of parting, during one of which Connal kisses the floor where Armida has walked and embraces the walls of the room where they are talking, Connal proposes—and Armida throws herself into his arms. He refuses to marry her until he is pardoned because he doesn't want to be accused of forcing Lord Montclare's daughter to marry a leader of banditti.

Desmond is in Wandesford's regiment, and he and Connal eventually meet in battle. Connal saves Desmond's life, and Desmond determines to fight and die with Connal since a rebel's brother can have no honor anyway. He is also depressed by the fact that his brief and idyllic marriage with Endymion (whose feminine name is Ines) had ended violently when Morosini discovered their elopement cottage. Both Ines and Morosini had fallen into the sea; Morosini's body was recovered, and there was no chance for Ines' survival. There is a last great battle in which the rebels are decisively defeated and dispersed; Wandesford's forces pursue the survivors.

The novel's denouement is characteristically violent and complicated. Lady Montclare decides that Desmond and Armida must marry, once again in order to seal Desmond's lips concerning

Endymion's sex. As with the act of parricide that Ippolito and Annibal are commanded to commit in *Fatal Revenge*, Desmond and Armida are persuaded in their weakened state to overlook their immediate horror at the idea, which to many people in the nineteenth century suggested a form of incest. Armida, however, takes a forty-eight-hour poison just before the ceremony. The ceremony is interrupted by the appearance of Ines, not dead but mentally deranged from the loss of her child after her plunge into the sea. In the meantime, Connal, on the way to a last meeting with Armida before her wedding to Desmond, has killed Wandesford in a duel. He is arrested as a rebel, tried, and sent before an execution squad. At the last instant, Desmond rushes into the line of fire and is also killed. Ines and Armida shortly die with screams of agony, and Lady Montclare expiates her sins in a convent.

A number of the incidents in *The Milesian Chief* are not necessary to the ultimate denouement, and I have not included these in the summary. Maturin was hard put to fill out four volumes. But, while this novel employs individual sequences that do not develop any of the characterizations or the plot, it has a relative advantage in not possessing the kind of digression that reduces *The Wild Irish Boy* to a potpourri of unrelated opinions and characters. The sequences themselves are effective—for example, Connal's plucking Armida from a runaway coach, and his saving her and Wandesford from drowning in a seastorm that anticipates great scenes in *Bertram* and in *Melmoth the Wanderer*.

The Milesian Chief would be a considerably more attractive tale than it is had Maturin been less disposed to resort to sentimental clichés of both action and diction. His heroes and heroines continually throw themselves at each other's feet; they turn away to hide faces brimming with tears; they are repeatedly confounded, horror-struck, or frenzied (with passion, curiosity, anger, or fear— fear for someone else, of course, never themselves); and they are thrown into consternation at each new plot development. But Maturin's talent for expressing poetic states of mind, which persists despite the hackneyed prose, compensates for some of the crudeness of plotting and diction. However foolish is the idea of the mistaken sex of Endymion, the steadily increasing intensity of the feelings of Desmond and Endymion for each other is coherently modulated in the sequence of their meetings. And, if we could over-

look the declamations and moral perfection of Connal and the
occasional full-blown emotings of Armida and her smug sense that
she is superior in the things that matter to Italians, we could
better perceive her depth of feeling and better appreciate her
remarkable independence from the world's opinion when she agrees
to share Connal's lot as a rebel.

It is doubly regrettable that Maturin often took refuge in rhetorical
clichés because, as *The Milesian Chief* demonstrates, he had a
sense of characterization that was in advance of his time. In most
eighteenth-century novels characters are static. In Fielding, Smollett,
Sterne—even in Samuel Richardson to some degree—characters do
not develop; they exist at the end of their novels much as they
had been at the beginning. They usually have a "humour"—a
dominating pattern of behavior: Tom Jones's high-spirited independent manliness, Tristram Shandy's whimsicality, Pamela's
and Clarissa's beleaguered virtuousness. Of the major characters
in eighteenth-century fiction, only Lovelace of Richardson's *Clarissa
Harlowe* stands out as a significant study of the psychological and
social forces that shape—and change—personality. Jane Austen,
of course, experimented with character development before Maturin
did, but her novels were held back from publication until after his
career had begun; and, in any case, we wonder what effect she could
have had on *The Milesian Chief.* It is not likely that the frenetic
Maturin would have read Austen with much absorption.

That Maturin was interested in change in personality is evident
in his first novel, *Fatal Revenge.* Even there, though, the final
personalities of Annibal and Ippolito are basically only intensifica-
tions of their original tendencies. Predictably, *The Wild Irish Boy*
has no more innovation in this regard than in any other. This
aspect of Maturin's development reaches its sudden peak in *The
Milesian Chief* and is responsible for the degree of permanent merit
that the novel possesses. Apart from Connal, none of the major
characters is without ambiguity; and, except for him, all experience
a development— some, naturally, more complex than others.[11]

For example, though Armida is surrounded by the false tone
that suffuses nearly every appearance of Connal, she is handled
with such care as to justify Maturin's intention (stated prematurely,
in the preface to *The Wild Irish Boy*) to delineate "female
characters and female interest." Her mental progress toward

suicide, though attended with overfrequent melodramatic situations, is plausible. Her vanity and arrogance, fostered by the effulgent praise of Italian society, are modified by the melancholy created by her father's odd behavior. By moving from the clamorous artificiality of Italy, which bores her, to the cold and lethargic skepticism of London society, which frightens her, she is made ready for the uncouth life of strong passions and desperate poverty of Ireland. The first ominous suggestion that her and Connal's love will lead to misery—the intuitive playing by Connal's blind Irish bard of the O'Morven funeral song—causes Armida's mind, "tinged by destiny and love," to assume "the gloomy colour of Connal's." Her mind is also affected by "a bleak wind [that] swept among the rocks" and by "the chill and cheerless air" that are characteristic of the west Ireland coast. By the time the battles between the rebels and the pursuing British army begin to take place, she can no longer command her energies of mind: "Her features spoke despair, not resolution." It is, then, no surprise when Lady Montclare takes her back into the palace following the defeat of the rebel army that Armida has lost her ambition and her imagination, nor that she has not the mental vigor to argue against her mother's false claim that she must marry Desmond to save Connal from death at the hands of Wandesford. Maturin is not as successful in taking Armida from one stage of her mental progress (or decline) to another as he is in depicting the individual stages; but there is no uncertainty in the presentation of Armida, and she becomes one of the most appealing people in Maturin's early fiction.

Desmond is nearly the equal of Armida as a characterization, if of a quite different sort. He partakes of the roguishness of youth that marks Tom Jones, and he is also a descendant of Smollett's picaresque heroes. He is as idealistic as Connal; but, when he thinks he has the opportunity to take advantage of Endymion's naïveté, he fully if shamefacedly intends to do so, furiously striking his brother when Connal tries to dissuade him. Again, though a sentimentalist in love, and knowing that Endymion is a female, he takes a mistress (the rejected Gabrielle, in fact) and leads a dissipated life in Dublin for a year before he and Ines elope. There are false tones to Desmond's character whenever he comes in contact with Connal, but by himself he is his own man. Perhaps it is because the physical aspect of love expressed so fervently by Desmond is closer

to the literary conventions of the twentieth century than is the
ethereally passionate but chaste love of Connal and Armida, but it
is only when Desmond appears that we seem clearly to be out of the
realm of romance and in that of realistic fiction.[12]

In the dedication to this novel, Maturin admitted that his first
two books were too far beyond "the reach of life, or the tone and
compass of ordinary feeling." He claimed that "If I possess any
talent, it is that of darkening the gloomy, and of deepening the sad;
of painting life in extremes, and representing those struggles of
passion when the soul trembles on the verge of the unlawful and the
unhallowed." Maturin continued in the dedication to say that in
his present book he has tried "to apply these powers to the scenes of
actual life," thinking that Ireland is a place where "the most wild
and incredible situations of romantic story are hourly passing before
modern eyes." Despite the passions and unusual situations in
The Milesian Chief, Maturin's dedication seems to be more a
rationale for his Gothic tales than for the particular book in hand.
Only Desmond, for example, "trembles on the verge of the unlawful and unhallowed"; Armida and Connal transgress only politically
and socially, not morally. The character of Lady Montclare would
offer excellent material for a study of conscience and despicable
behavior, but Maturin presents only her actions, not her feelings.
On the other hand, compared to the backdrops of *Fatal Revenge*,
those of *The Milesian Chief* represent, as the dedication implies,
"scenes of actual life."

CHAPTER 3

Experiments on the Stage

A S a playwright, Maturin finally achieved the popular success he had long sought. The theater in the early nineteenth century was in a debased state; Maturin's plays both participate in the debasement and rise above it at frequent points. Maturin constitutes one of the era's more noteworthy dramaturgical talents, for only "Monk" Lewis and Lord Byron wrote plays comparable to his in capturing the spirit of contemporary theater and in advancing the conventions of the stage. The conditions of the debasement of the theater rose inevitably from the history of the English stage since the Restoration period, and they go far toward accounting for the reception accorded Maturin's peculiar talent.

The Restoration stage was marked by witty criticisms of the conventional pieties that Cromwell's Puritan government had attempted to instill in the English population (partly by banning stage productions). In effect, such plays as William Wycherley's *The Country Wife* (1675), George Etherege's *The Man of Mode* (1676), and William Congreve's *The Way of the World* (1700) were attacks upon the common virtues. A natural post-Restoration reaction to this attack was the elaborate emotional support of the homely virtues, equally manifested in such diverse domestic genres as Richard Steele's comedy *Conscious Lovers* (1722), Colley Cibber's *Love's Last Shift* (1696), and George Lillo's tragedy *The London Merchant* (1731). This mood of support for virtue helps to account for the rise of sentimentality in fiction as well as in drama, and for the presence in many Gothic plays of lily-pure heroines.

A concomitant development from the Restoration's lack of reverence and of moral restraint was post-Restoration satire. Some of the propagandistic plays pretended to artistic detachment, like Joseph Addison's *Cato* (1713), which defended the principles of liberty during the tense days of Queen Anne's illness when there was no resolution yet made to the problem of succession. But the plays which were objected to the most strenuously by their victim-subjects were those which were bitter and outspoken. Henry Fielding wrote such plays as *Pasquin* (1736) and *The Historical*

Register for 1736 (1737)—plays recognizably directed against Prime Minister Robert Walpole. Partly to blunt the shaft of personal attacks, but also to prevent the growth of popular discontent against the Hanoverian government, Walpole forced the Parliament to pass the Licensing Act of 1737.

This act prohibited the production of original plays on any stage other than those of Covent Garden, Drury Lane, and the Haymarket, whose companies had been granted Royal Patents by Charles II and William III; and even these three London playhouses could be easily watched by the government. By requiring that every play be licensed by the Lord Chancellor, the act in effect banned seditious attacks on the government from the boards, as well as immoral and blasphemous productions. Walpole's purpose was accomplished: Fielding turned to fiction, the drama declined into harmless amusement for the illiterate masses, and the Hanoverians became constantly more solidly established.

Even though the Licensing Act was violated by many small theaters which operated despite their illegal status, the taste of the audience deteriorated. The audience during the Restoration had been composed almost entirely of aristocrats and courtiers; a later increase in the proportion of lower- and middle-class persons in the audience created demands for less verbalizing and for more direct appeal to the senses. Most of the theatrical productions during the late eighteenth century and Maturin's time were of several general types: comedy, burlesque, extravaganza, melodrama, farce, musical entertainments, and animal shows. Quite often all of the types were on the same showbill, one of the purposes being to evade the ban on legitimate drama by interlarding dramatic scenes with the other sorts of activity, another purpose being to keep from straining the attention span of the unsophisticated audience. Even legitimate plays in the licensed theaters leaned toward spectacular productions, with painted scenery and violent action, in order to attract audiences large enough to fill the cavernous buildings that their monopoly encouraged them to build. As if the situation were not already enough to turn would-be dramatists to other literary work, the Haymarket's productions consisted almost entirely of the lower forms of entertainment, leaving only Drury Lane and Covent Garden as possible sources of income for serious writers.

Accompanying the popularity of the spectacle was the emergence of the "star system." Previously the play alone had been the attraction for the audience, but in the eighteenth century certain players gained such eminence as to be in themselves a reason for people to see plays. The natural result was the formulation of histrionic tricks and practices that were brought to perfection in the virtuoso performances of actors such as David Garrick in the eighteenth century and such as Edmund Kean, John Kemble, and William Charles Macready in the nineteenth century. An almost standard practice was the lethargic underplaying of roles by the secondary characters in order that the impassioned gesturings, declamations, and movements of the stars would stand out the more brilliantly. Plays were seldom well rehearsed since only the performance of the star mattered to their success. In compensation for its deteriorative effect, the star system helped to preserve serious drama because the educated classes would visit the theaters primarily to see a great actor performing in verse dramas.[1]

Since only a limited number of orthodox, or legitimate, plays could be produced, there was little promise of a livelihood for aspiring playwrights.[2] The development of the novel in England owes a great deal to Fielding's biting wit and to Walpole's desire to remain at the head of a stable government, for the conclusive result of the confrontation between these two forces required writers to consider other channels of prose writing. With such exceptions during the last part of the eighteenth century as Oliver Goldsmith's *She Stoops to Conquer* (1773) and Richard Brinsley Sheridan's plays, little of permanent value was produced. English theatrical taste became so debilitated that Richard Cumberland (1732–1811), the author of innumerable hack sentimental plays, was esteemed highly enough that upon his death he was buried in the Poets' Corner of Westminster Abbey.

I *The Place of Maturin*

Maturin's plays are most accurately understood if we conceive of them as combining melodrama and the Gothic manner of stage presentation and as anticipating Romantic usages. His plays were written during the shift of emphasis from Gothic drama to melodrama as the most popular mode in the London theaters. In 1816 the two forms were barely distinguishable; and melodrama continued to use Gothic settings until well into the middle of the century; but separating them for discussion helps to indicate Maturin's place in the evolution of the two forms. There is also, of course, immense similarity between Gothic drama and Gothic fiction as I have briefly characterized it, and their antecedents are often the same; but they also have differing influences and conventions, because one is a public, the other a private, form of literary expression.

The origins of both melodrama and Gothic drama, like those of Gothic fiction, lie in the Elizabethan age, in William Shakespeare's *Macbeth* as well as in Thomas Kyd's *The Spanish Tragedy* and Christopher Marlowe's *Dr. Faustus*. Melodrama and the Gothic drama employ elements not only of the sentimental drama of Steele and Cumberland, with its emphasis upon delicacy of feminine sensibility, but also of the inflated and bombastic heroic drama of John Dryden and Nathaniel Lee of the Restoration period. Just as the heroic drama has heroes and villains more immense than life, so do the melodramas extol virtues and excoriate vices more unalloyed than normally found in real life. The heroic drama was also a natural stock on which to graft the musings about the horrific and unspeakable phenomena of which Horace Walpole, Ann Radcliffe, "Monk" Lewis, and Maturin were devotees.[3] Productions of plays with Gothic topics and treatment accompanied the interest in the supernatural and in romanticized antiquity that was exploited in the Gothic novel. (All of these Gothic novelists, incidentally, either wrote plays for the stage or saw their works adapted for theatrical production.)

The main features of Gothic drama are similar to those of the novel—the presence of architectural ruins; the gloom and remorse of the villain-protagonist; a shrinking female; a hero who is more effective by report than he is on-stage (often he is captured and imprisoned for most of the play); and a plot intended to create mystery and terror. An organic development within the Gothic drama is the progression of the man of evil from a loathsome villain, as he is in the early plays and in most of the Gothic novels, to a hero who attracts sympathy, which he finally clearly becomes in Lord Byron's plays. (This development has a reciprocal effect on the novel, as seen in Maturin's *Melmoth* and Mary Wollstonecraft Shelley's *Frankenstein*.)

Gothic drama developed earlier than melodrama into a fairly well-defined form during the latter part of the eighteenth century. It reached its peak with Maturin's plays, Byron's plays and closet dramas, and Percy Bysshe Shelley's *The Cenci* (1819; unproduced). After Gothicism declined, melodrama replaced it as the means to present in a forceful and colorful manner the conflict between good and evil. Gothicism is the more esthetically demanding form, for it attempts to employ a quality of language suitable for the horrible situations and emotions portrayed on the stage. Melodrama needs only stock speeches and gestures to go along with the pure evil of the villains and the pure virtue of its heroes and heroines. Melodrama's peak was achieved in the middle of the nineteenth century in the plays of Mark Lemon, the amateur theatrical productions of Charles Dickens, and the plays of Dion Boucicault. Though the melodrama was developed and "purified" after Maturin's time, its important characteristics were present while Maturin was writing. Maturin's own language often has a measure of the quality of cliché that we associate with later melodrama. Clichés, of course, are hardly rarities in Gothic writing; the point is that melodrama regularized the phrases, the contexts in which they were likely to appear, and the range of responses they were expected to elicit.

Maturin himself had no thought of writing anything so stereotyped as our conception of melodrama. He thought of himself as writing exalted poetic language and dealing with elevated characters whose dooms were portentous. Likewise, in the judgment of most of his audience and critics, as well as those of his literary advisers Walter Scott and George Lamb, he was writing high tragedy;[4] and he probably would have accepted the term "Gothic tragedian."[5]

Maturin's plays also provide an important element in the transition to literary Romantic drama, if a distinction may be drawn between Gothic and Romantic drama. Not all scholars allow such a distinction, but a tentative drawing of generic distinctions is often a helpful way to evaluate a writer's significance. Romantic drama is scarcely definable as a form; indeed, refusal to follow patterns makes up a considerable portion of the Romantic spirit. Many of the plays already indicated as examples of Gothic drama also possess the element that marks them as uncertain progenitors of Romantic drama—the protagonist's obstinate refusal to judge himself according to the dictates of normal morality. This "sign" of the main figure is set forth by Byron in *Manfred* and *Cain,* Shelley in *The Cenci,* and Maturin in *Bertram.* The difference between Gothic villain-heroes and Romantic heroes is one of often very subtle shading. Despite his evil ways, the Gothic villain-hero knows he sins and suffers remorse; the Romantic hero may be destroyed by his sins, but he sloughs society's imposition of morality, denying its applicability to his unique situation. The Romantic hero, then, is closer to the modern antihero than is the Gothic villain-hero. There are variations upon this Romantic element; for example, Manfred feels immense remorse for his unstated sin (evidently incest), but he refuses reconciliation with society. He remains independent at the price of eternal damnation, rejecting to the last instant the authority of morality.

Early Romantic dramas diverge substantially in only this way from the Gothic dramas. Gothic devices of the same general type are in Byron's dramas and in Maturin's *Bertram.* The central figures are possessed by inclinations to do what society would term evil, and they are either unable or unwilling to curb their amoral ambitions; as a result, they are set apart as uniquely demonic men. Maturin's hero and Byron's heroes are customarily sated and wearied by their experiences, and they long for no more experience and desire to escape the pains of continued life. But, though they express such a wish, Bertram and Byron's Cain are still energetic and capable of action. Maturin and Byron seem to have influenced each other, in addition to both taking ideas from the entire Gothic tradition and the spirit of Romanticism. Maturin's Bertram goes beyond the Giaour (1813) and Lara (1814) in his freedom from guilt; and Byron's Manfred (1817) benefits from the qualities of the hero Byron learned of while reading the manuscript of *Bertram.* (Byron left England in 1816 after reading *Bertram* in manuscript but before it was produced; he began writing *Manfred* later that year. He admitted the possibility of influence from many sources; but no critic has thought to connect *Bertram* with Byron's hero, a connection as likely in characterization as Part I of Goethe's *Faust* is in the dilemma faced by Manfred.)

Had Maturin continued in the Romantic manner in *Manuel* and in *Fredolfo* what he had begun in *Bertram,* he would belong more clearly in the front rank of Romantic dramatists. As it is, it seems that he did not really recognize the innovation he made in *Bertram;* or perhaps, as the example of *Fredolfo* suggests, he was unable to restrain his innovative instincts to one idea. In the two later plays he merely continued his borrowings from the many streams of dramatic tradition and erratically experimented with variations upon these traditions. He is, then, a contributor to the development of the drama, if an unheralded one; but he is not a master of any single form.[6]

II   Bertram *(1816)*

Maturin became interested in writing for the stage as part of his life-long search for a literary form that would bring him money. The immediate impetus was the 1814 success in Dublin of a mediocre play by a friend, Richard Lalor Sheil's *Adelaide; or, the Immigrants.* Evidently feeling that if a barrister could write a profitable play so could he, Maturin set to work. The resulting manuscript was sent to Walter Scott for a reading. Scott persuaded John Kemble to read it, but Kemble refused to produce the play.[7] In 1815 Lord Byron, on behalf of Drury Lane Theatre, asked Scott to write a play; but Scott instead referred Byron to Maturin's play. Byron was deeply impressed when he read *Bertram;* he sent a fifty-guinea loan to Maturin even before Edmund Kean agreed to play the title role or the other managers voted on the play. The manuscript was turned over to George Lamb, another of the Drury Lane's managers, for preparation for the stage. Bertram was a choice role for the star system, and it is one of the roles that Edmund Kean is still most famous for playing.

The play opened on May 9, 1816, and was the smash of the season, having over twenty performances. Maturin made nearly £1000 from the play including £350 for the book rights purchased by John Murray. Though most of the money went toward clearing away the massive debt for which he was liable, Maturin felt that with fame he had gained certain future prosperity. He brought in expensive furnishings for his house on York Street and gave and attended splendid parties. His spirits improved in manic fashion, and in this period he became notorious for his unclerical late-hour dancing, for his assiduous attendance at literary soirées in culture-barren Dublin, and for the extreme modes of his dress—in the highest fashion of pantaloons and tight black clothes one day; in the shabbiest apparel in his wardrobe the next.

The bubble did not last the year, and Maturin soon learned that he could not emulate his friend Walter Scott and live like a baron on literary expectations. But his reputation of eccentric extravagance persisted in the ensuing years of desperate penury—a reputation not wholly undeserved, for he was likely to dress his wife grandly on the receipt of payment for a new work. A more disturbing indication of his character in reaction to affluence is the decline in the performance of his religious duties. From the time *Bertram* was first produced, Maturin baptized no one until December 1, and married only one couple, on July 6, until September 9.[8]

At the apex of *Bertram*'s success, at the end of May, Maturin went to London at the invitation of Douglas Kinnaird of the Drury Lane management—his only known absence from Ireland, and he did not enjoy it, as I have already indicated. But he was at least spared from observing the conduct of the newly married Princess Charlotte and the Prince of Coburg, who, early in the play's run, entered during the middle of the last act. They had evidently come to enjoy the farce "The Maid and the Magpie," which followed *Bertram* that night, for they were "frequently in conversation during the remainder of *Bertram*."[9] Still, Maturin's admiration of titled persons was such that he probably would have experienced only delight that the heiress to the throne had come to his play at all.

The royal couple could well have given the play more attention. *Bertram* maintains a unified tone not possessed by either of Maturin's other plays. The poetry of *Bertram* is not as full-blown and extravagant as much of the dialogue in Gothic and Romantic drama; in fact, it is often relatively prosaic and straightforward. Nonetheless, there is plenty of frenetic activity, imparted through Maturin's stage directions, which have people fainting, falling backward into the arms of their menials, and bursting into tears. Bertram is frequently "dashing" and "throwing" people away from him. The poetry relies for much of its effect upon the necessity for expansive physical gesture required by the size of the theaters. One illustration from a naturally emotional scene may suffice. When the hero makes his identity known to the heroine by obscure references to his former appearance, she totters toward him and "(shrieks and

falls into his arms)." He then says, in a speech replete with opportunities for posturing:

> *Thus pale, cold, dying, thus thou art most fit*
> *To be enfolded to this desolate heart—*
> *A blighted lily on its icy bed—*
> *Nay, look not up, 'tis thus I would behold thee.*
> *That pale cheek looks like truth—I'll gaze no more—*
> *That fair, that pale, dear cheek, these helpless arms,*
> *If I look longer they will make me human.* (II.iii)

This first play of Maturin's combines several of the popular types
of stage performances. The play opens with a storm scene and a
shipwreck; and it contains the additional feature of a spectacle-
drama in its procession of knights in the fifth act. The same act
contains singing by monks, and earlier in the play there is a drinking song by bandits, both no doubt included to assuage the audience's expectation of music in plays. *Bertram* has no end of
Gothic dramatic conventions—a stormy seascape of seemingly
supernatural furor, a medieval castle and monastery, secondary
characters who express great fear for seemingly slight cause, a
heroine who hallucinates a gory corpse, and a hero-villain driven
by intense destructive energies.

Bertram's fiery deportment originates in his sense of being
wronged in having been expelled from his native Sicily and deprived of his estates and honors for ambitions against his king.
Having lost "high glory," he "recked not what was saved" and
became the leader of a group of bandits. But he has not lost his
noble bearing, and his "grandeur" is often remarked upon in the
play—in Maturin's stage directions, by Bertram himself, and by
other characters. Most remarkable among these testators to
Bertram's stature is the Prior, to whose monastery the gloomy and
diffident Bertram is brought when the ship carrying Bertram's
robber band is blown off course by a terrific storm and wrecked on
a rock off the coast of Sicily. The Prior knows all of Bertram's
history, for the monastery is adjacent to the estates which had formerly been Bertram's. These estates have been given to Lord
Aldobrand as a reward for saving Sicily from Bertram.

Despite the Prior's knowledge of Bertram's past, and despite
Bertram's frantically if vaguely worded threats upon Aldobrand's

life and family when he learns where he has come ashore, the Prior takes no effective precaution against Bertram's activities. Indeed, the Prior—who is characterized as at once doddering and saintly—is paralyzed by awe and admiration at Bertram's aspect. He promises not to betray Bertram—"Sorrow enough hath bowed thy head already/Thou man of many woes" (II.i)—and, rather than remain silent about the locale of the monastery, he repeatedly tells Bertram that "Hard by do stand the halls of Aldobrand/(Thy mortal enemy and cause of fall)." The Prior, more than any other character or feature of the play, encourages the equation of Bertram with Satan:

> *High-hearted man, sublime even in thy guilt,*
> *Whose passions are thy crimes, whose angel-sin*
> *Is pride that rivals the star-bright apostate's.* (III.ii)

The Prior's peculiarly inept behavior as an intermediary between Bertram and Aldobrand, and his a-Christian adulation of Bertram, are ethically inexplicable. The rationale is esthetic. The central character, to be played by a star actor, needs to have sympathy created for him. What better way to do this than having the kindly religious leader exonerate Bertram, in effect, from the charge of criminal malignity? Samuel Coleridge, who loathed *Bertram,* remarked ironically that he assumed, during the course of the play, that the Prior would turn out to be Bertram's father.[10]

Aldobrand's triumph has been made complete through his having married the girl Bertram had loved, and still loves, although the play gives only indirect indications that Aldobrand had ever associated the virtuous Imogine with Bertram. Bertram, on his part, does not know of Imogine's marriage until he meets her at Aldobrand's castle. Because Aldobrand is away from his castle taking part in a religious ceremony, Imogine performs the traditional courtesy of welcoming to the castle the "mariners" who have been saved from the storm. She still loves Bertram; before she learns he is on the island, she tells her attendant Clotilda that her heart is "Bertram's still, and Bertram's ever!" (I.v). But, though she had married Aldobrand only to save her father from starving, and though the marriage had been performed while she was under the influence of drugs, she has remained a "spotless wife" and a "too dutiful . . . daughter" (I.v).

Her virtue does not long survive the appeal that Bertram exerts on her. Even before he reveals his identity, her "fancy" is stirred by the "mystery of woe" about the shipwrecked mariner when she watches him from a distance (II.iii). Later, she is more concerned for Bertram's safety while he is in Aldobrand's territory than she is worried that Bertram might be planning to harm Aldobrand. Despite the melodramatic fortuitous appearance of her young son during two separate tense meetings with Bertram, which each time recalls Imogine to her married state and loyalties, she and Bertram arrange a final hour of parting. She distractedly reports the outcome of the meeting to Clotilda: "We met in madness, and in guilt we parted" (IV.ii).

Almost to a man, the reviewers remarked upon the forcefulness of the representation on the stage of the idea of infidelity.[11] None approved,[12] but sexual immorality, sadism, incest, and inversions of all sorts were common and indeed conventional elements in the widely popular Gothic drama. The extent of the moral outcry against *Bertram* must be attributed to the greater realism and to the sympathy shown the adulterers.[13]

Imogine's infidelity strains her reason, which snaps when Bertram kills Aldobrand in her sight. Bertram had sworn to Imogine that he would leave Sicily after their final meeting, but upon hearing that Aldobrand has returned home with a warrant from the king to seek him out and to execute him, he breaks into a fury and swears to kill Aldobrand.

Maturin's interest in psychological states is displayed to good effect in the progress of Bertram's attitudes toward Aldobrand. He had always hated Aldobrand; his resentment for his fall is directed against the man who had militarily defeated him. But, despite Bertram's early fulminations against Aldobrand, he seems content to let fierce but inactive resentment be his mode until his liaison with Imogine, which of course had never entered his plans since he had not known that she had become Aldobrand's wife during his exile. The chain of events that makes him determined to kill Aldobrand begins with the humiliating awareness that, by defiling Aldobrand's wife, he has both debased himself and erased the justification of his resentment against Aldobrand:

> *My fiend-like glory hath departed from me—*
> *Bertram hath nought above the meanest losel—*

> *I should have bearded him in halls of pride—*
> *I should have mated him in fields of death—*
> *Not stol'n upon his secret bower of peace,*
> *And breathed a serpent's venom on his flower.*
>
> .   .   .
>
> *Aldobrand—No—I never will forgive thee,*
> *For I am sunk beneath thee.* (IV.i)

His base seduction of Imogine has paradoxically deprived
Bertram of his stature of Gothic hero-villain, if only very temporarily.
The dialogue quoted above reveals the deterioration of Bertram's
Gothic self-concept. Sexual malfeasance has destroyed his sense
of persecuted superiority:

> *'Twas but e'en now* [i.e., before he learned of the king's
>   warrant], *I would have knelt to him*
> *With the prostration of a conscious villain;*
> *I would have crouched beneath his spurning feet;*
> *I would have felt their trampling tread, and blessed it—*
> *For I had injured him—and mutual injury*
> *Had freed my withered heart—* (IV.i)[14]

Thus Bertram reaches, though unwillingly and only briefly, a
psychological stage antecedent to personal and religious redemption. But with the news of Aldobrand's warrant from the king,
Bertram recovers his energies and hatred, his resentment churned
into action by the renewed official persecution by Aldobrand
("Hath he not pushed me to extremity?") and by the prospect of
making up for his unworthiness in having wreaked vengeance
through Imogine ("Lord Aldobrand, I [will now] brave thee in
thy halls [of pride]"). The progress of Bertram's attitudes toward
Aldobrand in this scene is a bit mechanical but dramatically well
paced nonetheless. There follows promptly Bertram's on-stage
murder of Aldobrand in Imogine's chamber in her presence.

Events come quickly and rather incoherently after Aldobrand is
killed. Bertram surrenders himself, after grandly cowing a roomful
of armed knights by brandishing his broken sword at them. He is
prepared to be executed for his deed, but he adamantly refuses to
express remorse. On the way to the place of execution, the knights,
monks, and Bertram come upon the insane Imogine, whose child
has just died, presumably by her hand. She asks Bertram to kill

her, by *"that hand [that] can deal death well"* (V.iii), but she then
expires quietly while gazing at him, so quietly that he does not
know immediately that she is dead. Finally realizing it, he snatches
a knight's sword and stabs himself. Unlike the customary Gothic
hero-villain of drama, Bertram does not employ religious cant at
his death. Although he asks the Prior and the knights to "lift up
your holy hands in charity" as he struggles in the agonies of
death, his concluding lines are given *"[with a burst of wild exulta-
tion]"*:

> *I died no felon death—*
> *A warrior's weapon freed a warrior's soul—* (V.iii)[15]

In effect, he praises suicide and denies that society can be the
appropriate punisher. This consistency of sternness aligns Maturin's
hero with those of Byron and Shelley, who are even more defiant
and unrepentant at their ends.[16]

The plot strains plausibility, as do the roles if taken as serious
representations of human beings or dramatic symbols. Almost all
of the characters manifest contradictory traits—some, such as
Bertram, functionally, but others, such as the Prior and Aldobrand,
in ways that blur their symbolic values in the matrix of the drama.
I have already referred to the Prior's unclerical praise of Bertram,
but equally out of keeping with the Prior's presumed saintliness
is his harshness toward Imogine. When Imogine, before her seduction, comes to him to confess her lawless love and hopefully to receive encouragement for chaste living, the Prior excoriates her
mercilessly:

> *Thou comest to me, for to my ear alone*
> *May the deep secret of thy heart be told,*
> *And fancy riot in the luscious poison—*
> *Fond of the misery we paint so well,*
> *Proud of the sacrifice of broken hearts,*
> *We pour on heav'ns dread ear, what man's would shrink from—*
> *Yea, make a merit of the impious insult,*
> *And wrest the functions of mine holy office*
> *To the foul ministry of earthly passion.* (III.ii)[17]

In other words, the Prior can tolerate Bertram's political rebellion, his threats of murder, and his lifetime of outlawry; but the

wife of the local liege lord and national hero gains neither his sympathy nor his time. After Aldobrand's death, Imogine again comes to the Prior and receives only his angry malediction (V.i). The Prior's role in feudal society, of course, suggests his bonds of fealty were closer to Aldobrand, whose honor is at stake, than to Aldobrand's wife; but this suggestion is contradicted by his failure to try to halt Bertram's schemes against Aldobrand. (There is no indication that he still considers Bertram, the former lord, in his feudal role.)

In all, the Prior functions as a "straight man"—he feeds lines to Imogine and Bertram to elicit Imogine's abjectness as a tormented woman and to emphasize Bertram's noble courage to face death unrepentant and unconfessed. He also serves as an index of how horrific events are: he faints while watching the shipwreck; nearly faints again when Bertram voices a desire to kill Aldobrand; and shrinks away in horror from Imogine's insane confession of complicity in Aldobrand's death. Part of the Prior's unstable behavior is explained by Maturin's distaste for Catholicism; for though the Prior may be saintly, he is jealous of the privileges of confession, and he is a posturing champion of his own invisible power. Critics have observed that his monastery is a scene of peace rather than a nest of deviltry as monasteries customarily are in Gothic literature,[18] but—to Bertram at least—it is also a place of stagnation and death-in-life (III.ii), a condition that Maturin develops in *Melmoth the Wanderer* as characteristic of monastic life.

Contradictoriness also affects Aldobrand in his relationship to the fatal ambitions of Bertram. According to Bertram, he had been unjustly exiled by "A despot's vengeance, a false country's curses" (II.iii). According to Aldobrand, Bertram had already rebelled before he himself acted; in fact, Bertram had triumphed over the king: "The craven monarch was his subject's slave—/ . . . From the state's vitals [I] tore the coiled serpent" (IV.ii). In all of his behavior seen by the audience, Aldobrand is broad-minded, conscientious, and considerate. To react to him as the strongman of a tyrant king, as Bertram pictures him, we must ignore the evidence Maturin presents directly. Still, there is some confusion about Aldobrand's nature: did he force Imogine to marry him, as she says; and if so, how can his gentlemanly behavior he evinces while actually on-stage be explained? It would seem that he, like the Prior, is valuable more as part of the plot machinery—that is, his role changes with the context—than as a representative of any intrinsic moral value.

The major points of interest in this play are its characterization of Bertram and its innovative use of the Gothic hero-villain convention. As the protagonist of a Gothic drama, Bertram embodies several conventions. The audience sympathizes with the Gothic hero-villain because the agony he suffers is "emphasized more heavily than the crimes that brought it."[19] Bertram has a heroine to terrorize; and the fact that he is opposed by a man of virtue (Aldobrand, despite the ambivalence about the wedding to Imogine) whose off-stage exploits are more effective than those he attempts on-stage further helps make him the dominant character in the play. Even though Bertram's capacity for destructive agony is not made fully evident until after he seduces Imogine, his despair and bitterness during the opening scenes adequately link him to the Gothic hero-villain.

But Bertram is more than just the result of the confluence of the elements of the Gothic dramatic tradition: he is an individual portrait, even though he follows certain patterns of the genre. His characterization has a vitality of development lacking in most Gothic villains, although his posturings and heroic speeches obscure the nature of this change. Most characters in Gothic drama are static. They have either committed their sins, such as the incest by the countess in Horace Walpole's *The Mysterious Mother,* or they commit them shortly after the play opens. *Bertram* is more subtle. The despair, which I mention above as connecting Bertram with the Gothic tradition, is not motivated by guilt, as is the despair of almost every Gothic hero-villain, but by a burning unrest of spirit and by an insatiable hatred of Aldobrand that it seems impossible to relieve by an act of revenge.

Gothic guilt is nearly absent in Bertram; not one of his actual actions is caused by a sense of moral guilt. He feels primarily only personal shame that his seduction of Imogine has violated the grounds of his self-concept, and news of the king's warrant totally disrupts this regret and his sympathy for Imogine. He feels no guilt or discomfort for his past political ambitions: "I was a man, I know not what I am—/What others' crimes and injuries have made me—" (II.i).[20] His justification for his murder of Aldobrand is equally free of self-recrimination: "He wronged me, and I slew him—" (V.ii). His sense of resentment and ill usage affects his every action in the play. He is quite dispassionate about seeing Imogine in Aldobrand's castle until he realizes that she is married to his enemy.

Thus, though Bertram is not wholly original, he is not simply an imitation of the guilt-ridden Gothic villain. While adopting from Gothic conventions the attributes of evilness and gloom in the protagonist, Maturin creates a unique context: the clergyman writes a play in which there is no religious repentance.[21] Bertram's remorse at the end may be Gothic in its representation of agony, but it is not Gothic in motivation. With great pride he refuses to regret his attempted subversion of the throne, his life of pillage, and his murder of Aldobrand. His remorse arises not from a sense of morality, as most Gothic dramatists and novelists felt to be necessary, but from psychological pressures. After he has wreaked his vengeance on Aldobrand, he relaxes, in effect, and is able to feel regret for having maddened Imogine.[22] (Just before he had killed Aldobrand, he could feel only a very modest pity for the disgraced Imogine: "My tiger spring must crush thee in its way,/But cannot pause to pity thee" [IV.ii].) Like Coleridge in *Remorse,* Maturin has a staunchly nonremorseful hero-villain until near the end. But Maturin's nonmoral method is innovative to a measure beyond Coleridge, whose hero finally undergoes the usual Gothic conversion to moral regret.[23]

Bertrand Evans does not consider *Bertram* in quite the manner in which I do, in two significant variations. He thinks that Bertram feels guilt at the very opening of the play and that this Gothic guilt is without foundation. Evans believes that Bertram does no wrong until after the play has begun, contrary to the usual Gothic hero, including Byron's heroes, who have done wrong before the plays' actions, which thus are movements toward the revelation of the heroes' *past* unspeakable sins. "Bertram, before the early scenes, which show him tormented, had committed no crime. . . . Bertram, then, if the foolish truth must be stated, suffers because he is the kind of hero who suffers."[24]

To put it a different way, Evans believes that Bertram suffers from guilt feelings just because he is a Gothic protagonist—that Maturin is, in a pointedly grotesque way, subservient to the traditions of the genre. But, as I have shown, Bertram's conscience at the beginning is by far the least important factor in his mood. The Prior says in a monologue that Bertram is a guilty person (III.ii), but Bertram does not *himself* say anything that indicates he accepts guilt for any other activity than being misanthropic. His startings, twitchings, and fearful aspect reveal his Gothic obsessiveness, but the rest of his actions make clear that it is not guilt that obsesses him but resentment for his outcast condition.

Bertram has committed sins, however, for which guilt feelings would be appropriate. The fallacy in Evans' theory that Bertram's guilt feeling is without cause lies in his failure to observe Bertram's criminality in political matters as well as his being the chieftain of a band of murderers and thieves. Evans' view of Bertram's initial sinlessness also does not take into account Imogine's testimony of the effect Bertram's activities in exile have had upon him:

> High glory lost he recked not what was saved—
> With desperate men in desperate ways he dealt—
> A change came o'er his nature and his heart
> Till she that bore him had recoiled from him,
> Nor know the alien visage of her child. (I.v)

Thus, whether we accept Bertram's or Aldobrand's version of Bertram's political actions, it is clear that Bertram's character is not merely a residue from his ancestors in the Gothic drama. Any other Gothic hero would be guilt-ridden by Bertram's background; Bertram grandly ignores the despicableness of his behavior to declare his high passions, and that is his uniqueness in the Gothic tradition of guilt.[25]

Much more might be said about *Bertram*. For example, Imogine comes close to being a Gothic heroine-villainness. Her wedding was done with a "ministering demon" mocking the "robed priest,/With some dark spell, not holy vow" (II.iii), and her expression of remorse after her infidelity is in the best Gothic manner:

> Whom doth the dark wind chide so hollowly?
> The very stones shrink from my steps of guilt,
> All lifeless things have come to life to curse me:
> Oh! that a mountain's weight were cast on me;
> Oh! that the wide, wild ocean heaved o'er me;
> Oh! that I could into the earthy centre
> Sink and be nothing. (IV.ii)

This speech strikes me as another innovation by Maturin—a heroine equivalent to a hero-villain, rather than one merely persecuted by him. If such a paralleling were Maturin's intention, he is only partially successful. Imogine is Bertram's equal in passion, but her passion is sentimental rather than stark or obsessive. She may have preserved Bertram's portrait through the years and mooned over it at every opportunity, but Bertram's pursuit of her is more than she has the resilience to cope with. In that her final ranting insanity is of a piece with her romantic preservation of her ideal of the exiled Bertram, Maturin develops a unified psychological portrait. She obviously has a weak mind, unsettled by a long battering by memory and by the sudden appearance of immense temptation in the person of Bertram. But she is less interesting toward the end of the play; there she is basically a device to create a crescendo of emotion before the curtain. Still, the power in her role as a whole is probably the reason for Edmund Kean's objection to reviving the play in subsequent seasons as often as its reputation would have seemed to demand: Imogine provides too much of a second focus of audience attention, thereby detracting from the role of Bertram.[26]

Despite the flaws that arise from the unresolvable contradictions within the genre and from weaknesses in Maturin's own creativity, *Bertram* rewards attentive reading. Its poetry has only a few impressive and restrained utterances that accord with today's tastes, and the play certainly would not bear a new production. But it deserves to be read with *Manfred* and *The Cenci* in courses in drama and Romantic writers.

Some attention must be given to the deletions from the original manuscript recommended by Scott and by Byron and accomplished by George Lamb.[27] The principal deletion is that of the "dark knight of the forest," presumably an agent of Satan. He is never on-stage; but his presence in the woods near Aldobrand's castle, referred to by several characters, creates a mood of mystery complementary to Bertram's earlier political motivations and his present desire for revenge. This specter's exhortations reinstills Bertram's destructive tendencies—

> *Forgotten thoughts of evil, still-born mischiefs,*
> *Foul fertile seeds of passion and of crime,*
> *That wither'd in my heart's abortive core,*
> *Rous'd their dark battle at his trumpet-peal;—*

tendencies which lead to the murder of Aldobrand. The effect of the alterations is at once to make Bertram's actions seem more narrowly motivated and to make more realistic the actual representation of action. Bertram's murder of Aldobrand is carried out in the produced version because of a sudden rearousal of long resentment at learning that Aldobrand has a warrant from the king to arrest him. In the manuscript the reasons for the murder of Aldobrand are much less clear: Bertram's interview with the dark knight comes immediately after he has learned of the king's warrant, but the interview does not strengthen his resolve to kill Aldobrand so much as it adds ineffable "forgotten thoughts of evil" to resentment as the driving forces in Bertram's act of murder.

Some of the deleted passages are given by Walter Scott in his review of *Women*. Scott felt that even an indirect representation of an evil spirit was unsuitable for the stage.[28] But the deletion is neither desirable nor undesirable in itself; Scott's argument did not have total validity even in his own day. "Real" ghosts appeared in the dramatizations of Radcliffe's *Romance of the Forest* (1794; under the title of *Fountainville Forest*) and in "Monk" Lewis' *Adelmorn, the Outlaw* (1801) and *Wood Daemon* (1807) without harming the plays' successes. To my mind, *Bertram* would be a stronger play if it retained the evil spirit. Such genuine supernaturalism would have accorded more clearly with Maturin's genius, as Maturin wrote to Scott.[29] But the published form has essential unity and coherence; the revision was skillfully made.

III   Manuel *(1817)*

Manuel (1817) is Maturin's only work that was written to order. Edmund Kean requested that Maturin provide him with the role of a madman, since a production of *King Lear* was thought to be impolitic while George III was ill. Writing hastily to capitalize on the success of *Bertram*, Maturin's creativity atrophied and he produced a work only faintly reminiscent of either *Lear* or *Titus Andronicus*. Kean could bear to deliver the role with his customary energy only once—he merely walked through the play in the other five performances which it received.[30] Since the author's rights did not begin until the ninth performance, Maturin did not receive a penny from the production;[31] but out of kindness the publisher

Murray let him have all of the profits from the publication of the play. Murray did not publish anything else by Maturin.

In the narrative, Manuel is a Cordovan nobleman who had lived well into middle age before his son Alonzo was born, whose birth disinherited Manuel's kinsman, De Zelos. When Alonzo fails to return from a military triumph over the Moors, Manuel immediately accuses De Zelos of murder. He cannot prove De Zelos' guilt, although De Zelos' agitation and guilty apprehensiveness make it obvious that he is responsible for Alonzo's absence. When a trial by champions is arranged, Torrismond, De Zelos' stalwart son who is in love with Manuel's daughter Victoria, fights for his father. A mysterious black knight appears at the last instant to fight for Manuel; the knight is defeated; but, in his dying moments, he gives to Ximena, De Zelos' daughter, a sheathed dagger on which is inscribed the name of the murderer of Alonzo, with the admonition that the dagger should be unsheathed only in the presence of judges. Ximena is delighted, for she assumes that the dagger will clear her father of all suspicion. But, when Torrismond unsheathes the dagger, the name on the blade turns out to be De Zelos'; the knight had been hired by De Zelos, and his conscience had smitten him after he had killed Alonzo.

One of the criticisms of the original manuscript of *Bertram* which Walter Scott and George Lamb had made to Maturin was the length of time that elapses between the murder of Aldobrand and the end of the play. As if to atone for this lapse in *Bertram,* Maturin ends *Manuel* within a page of the revelation that De Zelos is the murderer. In the bloody aftermath of the revelation, Torrismond attempts to kill himself for being, though unwittingly, a parricide in revealing his father's crime; De Zelos stabs himself; and Manuel, who dies in delirium, rants about De Zelos' tortures at the hands of "fiends."

In Maturin's eagerness to satisfy Kean, critics, and audiences, he borrowed from a range of sources but included little of himself. Even the scenes of fear and revelations of secrets, Maturin's forte in his novels, employ strained sentiments expressed in trite language. The play's inflated rhetoric and its Spanish-Moorish locale, common to Dryden's verse dramas, link the play inorganically to the heroic tradition; the references in scene settings to Gothic architecture and ruins, as well as the frenetic personality of De Zelos, evince the play's borrowings from the materials of Gothicism. The artificiality of the play's utilization of Gothicism is nowhere so clear as in Victoria's fear of the family castle to which Manuel is exiled after the trial by combat (which temporarily "proved" he had falsely accused De Zelos); and the justification for her attitude is solely a requirement imposed by the genre. Her superstitious musing bears upon nothing in the action, but it does help to create the atmosphere of desperation in which the play concludes:

> *Dark walls our prison, and perhaps our tomb?*
> *The voice of by-gone time, that sweeps your confines,*
> *Murmurs of deeds long buried in its lapse;*
> *Each step I print upon your marble floor*
> *Seems as it trod the unexplored dwelling*
> *Of some unearthly tenant, whose roused voice*
> *Peals on the thunder of the answering echoes,*
> *To bid me pause*—(V.i)[32]

Acts ending in dumb-show tableaux, the grimaces by the villain De Zelos, and his "Old Bailey self-betrayals, by which conscious guilt is made to say more than it intended"[33] are characteristics of the melodrama. If the characteristics of De Zelos can be traced to melodrama and Gothicism, those of Manuel come directly from Classical tragic theory and from Elizabethan example. Manuel deserves to suffer, for he has elevated his son above his due importance, as Manuel's confessor states:

> *He loves him as no earthly thing should be,*
> *In the scale of duty, lov'd—makes him a god*
> *Shrined in his heart, and does him worship there*—(I.i)

Along with Greek-like indifference to offending the gods, Manuel possesses arrogance toward possible machinations of his enemies. Upon the birth of his son, he began to treat De Zelos carelessly, taking no trouble to moderate De Zelos' bitter disappointment and encouraging the coldness of his courtiers toward his former heir. Like King Lear, Manuel is not open to experience or wisdom until it is too late to do anything but suffer for his shortsightedness.

One of the reasons for the self-centered Kean's disenchantment with the play could well have been his discovery, during the first performance, that Manuel's was not the only strong role, and indeed was not even the center of interest, except for the energy implicit in his ravings in the last act and the generally solid dialogue in the first and third acts. De Zelos is a far more colorful and engrossing figure. He is the consummate Gothic-melodramatic villain, with no possibility of being considered a hero-villain like Bertram. His malign hate for Alonzo had begun at Alonzo's birth; but, during Alonzo's lifetime, he pretends to be indifferent to his poverty and to the scorn of his acquaintances. Nonetheless he complains constantly to his children about the coldness and hypocrisy of his former flatterers. He refuses to allow his chivalrous son Torrismond to become a warrior in Alonzo's army because he cannot afford to outfit him grandly enough. His displays of fear and hatred are stereotypical, but they nevertheless afford opportunities for more complex acting than the direct ravings of Manuel.

Torrismond, also, diverts attention from Manuel, although hardly in a way that improves the play. Torrismond has many changes of heart in a single scene, and each change offers him a chance to declare his wholehearted allegiance to a different ideal. He initially suspects his father of killing Alonzo, and is hesitant about fighting in a trial for a false cause; his father calls him a coward, which causes him to start *"(as if from a trance)"* and rush forward threateningly, only to recognize his father and fall on his knees. He *"(bursts into tears)"* in his agony; and, when his father scornfully says he will serve as his own champion, Torrismond ecstatically shouts his father's innocence upon the proof that he would not "risk a deathless soul's perdition!" and he kneels to kiss his father's hands. When Victoria tells him that Manuel has no champion and intends to fight for himself, Torrismond promises to *"spare the ruin* [Manuel]," and he presents Victoria his sword *"(with enthusiasm)."* But the sound of trumpets recalls him to his duty: *"Have I not sworn?— Have I no father too?"* His wild determination to fight for his father again flags when Victoria tells him that "The shield of Manuel is his daughter's breast," and he *"(rushes to throw the sword at her feet),"* but another sound of trumpets causes him to retrieve the sword and rush off the stage to conclude the scene (IV.i). Such shallow indecisiveness and bombast in the play's most conventionally chivalric character could scarcely add to the dignity of Manuel's next appearance.

The ludicrousness of Maturin's conception of character in this play is clear enough from Torrismond's diametric and erratic reactions to each new appeal to his emotions—seven in the one scene alone. The laxity of Maturin's attention to the plot is attested by the device of revealing the murderer. It is fantastic that a man shown to be so cunning and patient a schemer against Alonzo as to wait two decades before finally putting a plan into execution would be absentminded enough to give the assassin his personal weapon, let alone one that contained his name on the blade. As a contemporary reviewer remarked about this device, "[The play] should have been a comedy."[34]

IV   Fredolfo *(1819)*

The writing of *Fredolfo* followed closely upon that of *Manuel,* but it was not produced until 1819 after the novel *Women* had been published. George Lamb had left the Drury Lane Theatre, which was suffering from internal dissension and a lack of good performers; but he recommended Maturin's play to the management of Covent Garden Theatre, which accepted it after reading only the first act. It is conceivable that the delay in production occurred because the management then read the rest of the play. Lamb had warned Maturin not to make the first act too good, for the "principal fault" of *Manuel* had been the inability of the rest of the play to satisfy the expectations created by the first act;[35] but Maturin's inspiration and control again failed him by the third act of *Fredolfo.*

In March and April, when the play was in rehearsal in London, Maturin was in Dublin, harassed by the difficulty of writing enough sermons to complete the volume that Archibald Constable had already paid for and which was published later in the year. He was being pressed by Constable as well to furnish copy for *Tales,* later to be called *Melmoth the Wanderer,* for which he had received a large advance. But the anxiety he felt to finish these two works was alleviated by his confidence that he would be established as a major writer with the success of *Fredolfo.*

Unfortunately, he miscalculated the quality of the play he had sent to London. If a stage success were as important to his future as he wrote Constable it was, he would have been well advised to

have gone to London to improve it. As it was, the play experienced
severe rehearsal difficulties; and its production was announced and
postponed at least twice. When it finally was produced in mid-May,
it closed after only one performance, though it had Macready in
the role of Wallenberg, the villain, and Charles Kemble as Adelmar,
the conventional hero. According to the producer, Alaric Watts,
the play was literally laughed and shouted off the stage. None of the
actors liked his part because, as with *Manuel,* the parts were too
equal in importance. One of the bit players, catching the infection
of dissatisfaction from the stars, delivered in a stolid manner the
supposedly frenzied line, "Our lord!—our lord! the storm! he
perishes!" (I.i). After that early point, the audience took nothing
seriously until Wallenberg stabbed Adelmar with a surrendered
sword (V.ii), an act which outraged the British sense of fair play,
and the production ended in tumult.[36] Maturin's hopes for financial security landed him in greater distress than before, since his
dreams of writing another success like *Bertram* had caused him to
neglect *Tales* and thus to strain the patience of Constable, who
thereafter insisted upon having a manuscript in hand before sending any payment to Maturin.

The failure of *Fredolfo* must have been the more disappointing
to Maturin because the situation of the play is the most promising
dramatically of all of Maturin's plays. The play employs the social
background of the Swiss struggle in the fourteenth century for independence from Austria; several characters trapped in situations
not worthy of their essential natures; and the suspenseful threat of
malign political and personal persecution. But the plot's coherence
is seriously rent by uncreative devices intended to sustain interest
as the play progresses: numerous redundant, abject pleas for mercy
by the heroine Urilda, and Wallenberg's nefarious schemings. And
the rhetoric throughout is wildly flamboyant.

Fredolfo is a hero of the Swiss people because he had resisted
the Austrian conquest of their country, but he has nursed for years
a secret guilt. On returning from his last campaign ten years before
the time of the play's action, he had discovered that his wife had
been raped by the Austrian governor Wallenberg and had drowned
herself. With the assistance of a deformed servant Berthold,
Fredolfo had waylaid Wallenberg in the mountains and had killed
him. As a result, he loathes himself morally; moreover, he is afraid

of being punished through the falseness of Berthold, and of being recognized by a young mountain lad, Adelmar, who had tried to prevent the murder of Wallenberg. Basically a noble and kind man, Fredolfo retains Berthold in his employ; and he merely sends Adelmar abroad and hires agents to prevent him from returning. Adelmar cannot understand why the national hero Fredolfo dislikes him, and remains dedicated to him. Somehow, despite being in exile, he also manages to fall in love with Fredolfo's daughter Urilda, who returns his affection.

The play begins with Adelmar and Wallenberg's son, the present governor, both coming to Fredolfo's mountain castle, which he himself is visiting for the first time since he had killed the elder Wallenberg nearby. The first act gives background information at the same time that it shows Adelmar saving both Urilda's and Fredolfo's lives from a mountain flood; and the second act presents first Berthold's and then Wallenberg's proposals to Fredolfo for Urilda's hand in marriage. He angrily rejects Berthold, and he allows Urilda herself to answer Wallenberg, which she does as a free Swiss girl flinging aside a tyrant's insult. The act closes as the disappointed Berthold tells Wallenberg, who is choked with fury at Urilda's statement, that he can tell him who killed his father. As the two leave together, Fredolfo's anguished "Lost! lost! Oh, God, for ever!" brings down the curtain. These first two acts are compact and directive; and we can anticipate powerful confrontations in the succeeding acts.

There are indeed confrontations in the remaining three acts, but they are carried out in a ranting and passionate manner that nullifies the effect of the initial two acts. Wallenberg arrests Fredolfo and threatens to execute him, despite Urilda's frantic pleas. Wallenberg's awareness that the stalwart, patriotic Adelmar is a threat to Austrian power deepens the effect of his jealousy of the Swiss lover of Urilda. Knowing also that Adelmar will risk any danger to save Fredolfo, Wallenberg schemes with Berthold to capture the young man. Urilda, through their promise to offer only a token resistance and through her terror for her father's life, is persuaded to sign a plea to Adelmar to storm the castle to rescue Fredolfo. Wallenberg and Berthold intend to overwhelm Adelmar's forces and then to enjoy Urilda's shrieks as she watches Wallenberg torture both Adelmar and her father to death.

But Adelmar is successful. Fredolfo is rescued, but Adelmar is forced to leave Urilda within the sanctuary of a monastery while he seeks additional men-at-arms. Wallenberg, who arrives at the monastery before Adelmar returns, violates the right of sanctuary. While Wallenberg holds a knife to Urilda's throat, first Fredolfo and then Adelmar give their swords to Wallenberg. Treacherously, Wallenberg stabs Adelmar with his own sword. But as Wallenberg stands *"[in malignant stupefaction at the spectacle of Urilda's despair],"* Fredolfo stabs him:

> *Villain! let Vengeance pay her triple debt!*
> *This for the sire—the mother—and the child!*

Urilda, insane with grief and horror, delivers a last speech and then *"[falls on the body of Adelmar, and expires slowly, forcing a smile as she sees her father's agony]."* Although the play breaks down after the second act, there are sections that should be effective on the stage. Many speeches throughout have energetic and strong phraseology, but the farfetched sentiments that are expressed make reading the play an exercise in tolerance. Wallenberg's and Berthold's efforts to convince Urilda to sign the plea to Adelmar gain tension when Wallenberg indicates that he pities her (an indication surely plausible to a girl who has always been admired by men) and when Berthold refuses to swear that he is not preparing a trap. Berthold further insinuates that, if Urilda does not stop questioning his sincerity, her father might mount the scaffold sooner than scheduled. Another effective bit of stage work, one that echoes previous Gothic plays, is Fredolfo's relief upon finally being captured: he repents his acts, but he still is torn between eagerness to die and inability to pray. His confession to Urilda that he is indeed guilty of a foul murder makes good drama through the devices of sentimental convention, as she first refuses to believe him and then loyally declares her firm love for him. But even these scenes employ too frequently the distraught and fantastic language that dominates the play; and the stage directions indicate that the characters continually throw themselves about the stage in postures of despair, fear, outrage, and so forth.

The ranting and posturing in *Fredolfo* is so excessive that we might wonder whether Maturin is trying to mock thespian conven-

tions of expressive gesture and inflated delivery—though, given
Maturin's need for money and his hopes for this play, we know that
he certainly was writing what he thought his audience would ap-
plaud. For instance, Urilda is an extremely intense young lady
throughout. Her customary deportment is typified by her plea for
mercy for her father from the villainous Wallenberg:

> Urilda. [Falling on the ground] *He is—my father!*
> Wallenberg. *Prostrate at my feet!*
> *The flower that scorn'd the touch must court the tread—*
> *Rise, lady, rise! you much debase yourself*
> *To clasp the knees of a rejected wooer!*
> Urilda. [Writhing at his feet in agonizing humiliation]
> *Let not my gracious lord in wrath remember*
> *The frantic folly of a wayward girl!*
>   . . .
> *How can you crush a worm, to see it writhe?* (III.iii)

Only moderately more frenetic than this is her dying speech, the
last speech of the play. Adelmar has just died in her arms; her fatal
grief is colored by hallucinations:

I deem'd that it [life] *was past—but still I'm here—*
Chain'd down in torture—struggling with a fiend!—
                                 [Pushing away her father.]
Avaunt! thy touch is fire—my veins are scorched!
I blaze!—I blaze!—stand off!—pour rivers o'er me!
                                      [Shrieking.]
Ah! with hot gore ye drench me—I'm o'erwhelmed!
A sea of blood!—down, down, amid the billows!
Down, down for ever!—rest is at the bottom! (V.ii)

Wallenberg too is given to frenzy and to maliciousness, and he is
motivated partly by revenge for his father's murder and partly by
furious pride at having been rejected by the initially imperious
Urilda; but his emotions create not sympathy but revulsion. The
writers of the Gothic stories seldom explicitly develop the nature
of the psychological aberrations they bestow upon their villains,
but it is obvious that Wallenberg's perversity is sexual, that he is
a sado-masochist as much as he is representative of demonic evil.

    The characterization of both Berthold and Wallenberg suggests
a quality of intuitive psychological understanding on Maturin's

part that appears to some degree in all of his works. Wallenberg remains agonized by his love for Urilda, and he finds he can forgive her anything—even her refusing his proposal and shrinking from him—except loving someone else. Similar to Wallenberg in exciting moral loathing, Berthold as a personification of evil is a powerful element in the play. He is physically ugly and totally amoral. Indispensable to Fredolfo because he had assisted in the killing of the elder Wallenberg, he has bided his time to claim his reward, which he voices (in a suitably revolting manner) as a desire to marry Urilda. He is similar to Shakespeare's Richard III in that his hatred toward all is activated by his deformity, and he is linked as well to Shakespeare by his Iago-like malignity toward his master.

As with *Bertram* and *Manuel,* one cannot find all of *Fredolfo*'s qualities in a single genre. Wallenberg and Berthold are drawn as much from melodrama as from Gothicism, and Adelmar and Fredolfo present still more uncertain amalgams. Wallenberg allegorizes evil pursuing virtue. Berthold possesses the innate malignity toward Fredolfo characteristic of Gothic villains, but his symbolic deformity and ugliness place him clearly in the melodramatic tradition, which employs physical appearance as an index to moral quality. Villainy in Gothic literature, on the other hand, tends to come in amorphous and unremarkable physical forms, with ominousness in manner rather than in appearance, or in deceptively attractive forms, such as Count Montoni in *The Mysteries of Udolpho,* the temptress "monk" of *The Monk,* or Melmoth. Adelmar is a "child of woe,/Of persecution, and of mystery" (I.i), like Byron's protagonists, but, since he is of spotless virtue and manliness, his woefulness and the persecution he suffers make him more akin to the waif and the cheated rightful heir of melodrama than to Byron's Lara, or to Maturin's own Bertram. In Adelmar, then, we have the insipidity of the Gothic hero-lover and the lamentative paranoia of the protagonist of a Byronic drama—and it is easy to understand why the qualities do not coalesce.

Fredolfo's guilt associates him with the Gothic hero-villain; but he is too humane to be a clear-cut Gothic figure; he releases Adelmar, despite Berthold's eagerness to cut the young man's throat, with a phrase that indicates that he possesses only intermittently the Gothic manner and obsessions: "Though one wild moment's sudden agony/Made me a fiend, I am a man again" (II.i).

Like Bertram and Lewis' Adelmorn, Fredolfo is a development upon the Gothic hero-villain convention. Like Bertram, he will attack a foe (the elder Wallenberg), but not "him I've injured [Adelmar]" (II.i). And, after all, his murder of Wallenberg is justifiable on personal, marital, and folkloristic grounds. What is reprehensible about it is that he did not attack Wallenberg in single combat or give him any choice of weapons and ground. In all, Fredolfo's role is potentially the best-rounded and most realistic of any in Maturin's plays; his plight is more tragic and compelling than Bertram's; he attracts a natural sympathy. But the wild rhetoric and frenzied stage action of *Fredolfo* makes the play less satisfactory than *Bertram,* where the language and stage action are more consonant with Bertram's alienated personality.

V   *Other Dramatic Writings*

Maturin also wrote *Osmyn, the Renegade; or, the Siege of Salerno,* possibly at the same time he was writing *Fredolfo,* but it was never published. Maturin had first hoped that it and *Fredolfo* would be produced simultaneously at Covent Garden and Drury Lane. But its production was doubly delayed by Maturin's tardiness in finishing the last three acts and by Edmund Kean, for whom Maturin had written the lead role. Kean, who held the manuscript for years, avoided the requests for its return made by Alaric Watts, to whom Maturin had entrusted it; but Kean's action was not uncommon in his career as unscrupulous actor-manager. *Osmyn* was finally produced by Macready in Dublin in 1830 with moderate success. The author's share went to Maturin's widow.

All that is known about the play is based on a summary of the plot in the *Edinburgh Literary Journal* and the printing of a few passages in the *Dublin Literary Gazette* and in the *Irish Quarterly Review*.[37] Osmyn, a Christian count, has been unjustly deprived of his estates and honors by Manfred. Years afterward, to obtain revenge, Osmyn joins Turkish forces besieging a Christian town, Otranto. Like Bertram, then, he returns to his native lands as an invader; and, like Bertram, he is propelled by resentment rather than guilt. Osmyn succeeds in capturing Guiscard, who he thinks is the dead Manfred's son; and he decides to sell him into slavery. But Osmyn's wife Matilda, who had not gone into exile with him and who after Manfred's death had publicly pretended to have been married to Manfred, reveals that Guiscard is really Osmyn's son. Osmyn thereupon releases his son and is killed by the angry Turkish commander.

There is little ostensible Gothicism in the plot other than the names of Manfred and Otranto, but the language partakes of the Gothic inflation observable in Maturin's other plays. Osmyn expresses, in one passage, his resentment at Matilda for supposedly turning to Manfred after his own banishment:

> Oh! when the tide of ruin swept my towers,
> Whom did I grasp at in the wreck?—that woman!
> Whom did my last appealing groan invoke?
> Whom did my bursting eyeballs strain to see—
> (Would they had burst)—whom did the blood I shed
> Drench to her shrinking bosom?—that—that woman!

Osmyn himself seems strikingly like Bertram, and his relationship to the Gothic convention is as ambivalent as Bertram's and Fredolfo's. He is the destructive hero-villain, who, even more than Fredolfo, is more sinned against than sinning.

"The Sybil's Prophecy: A Dramatic Fragment" was published after Maturin's death, probably extracted from his papers by his wife for the sake of whatever money it would bring. Upon Maturin's death, Walter Scott had promised Mrs. Maturin that he would edit her husband's unpublished works as a memorial, she to receive all of the profits. The bankruptcy in 1826 of Scott's business partners, and his moral obligation to pay off more than £100,000 in debts, prevented him from fulfilling his promise. Mrs. Maturin managed to publish only a few pieces. "The Sybil's Prophecy" is one of Maturin's more restrained Gothic pieces, but we cannot know, of course, whether the rest of the play would have been in the same manner as this single scene. It treats of a girl and her lover who visit a mysterious woman who lives in a cave and who is known to be a prophetess; she predicts that they will be married only in death (a typical Gothic phrase). The concluding lines of the fragment imply strongly that the woman is the girl's long-lost mother, who years before had vanished during a trip through the region containing the cave.

Frequently in these discussions of Maturin's plays, I have suggested Maturin's reactions to Gothic, Byronic, Romantic, and melodramatic influences and traditions, and his frequent progressiveness in employing the conventions of these forms. The point is not that Maturin was remarkably inventive, or that he is an unrecognized touchstone in the development of English theater. If anything is remarkable, it is his absorptive ability to borrow from all of the active traditions in producing his singular effects. The lesson of Maturin should be instructive in pointing out the difficulty of "placing," in a final sense, any writer in the development of his genre.

Some critics give Maturin large credit for the collapse of Gothic drama, and they argue that the moral iniquity of *Bertram* and the rhetorical excesses of *Manuel* and *Fredolfo* revolted the audience and rendered them intolerant of Gothicism. A more likely explanation is that Maturin came at the end of a long-lived fashion that was inevitably destined for the decadence with which he supplied it.

CHAPTER 4

A Last Try at "Real Life"

MATURIN had indicated in the preface to *The Milesian Chief* that he was ready, in 1812, to describe "scenes of actual life." And he tried his best, working to diminish his natural bent toward the horrific in that novel though retaining a sensational plot. In the 1818 preface to *Women; or, Pour et Contre* he admits that the failure of his three previous novels was accounted for by their lack of reality and "*vraisemblance.*" The present book, he says, is drawn more from experience; and, he adds, its sole interest is the reality of its characters.

Maturin's prefaces tend to be self-deprecating, as if he were perpetually balancing the demands of art against the indifference toward literary quality prerequisite of a priest who still harbored the least hope of preferment. The published preface replaces an earlier one which the publisher, Archibald Constable, thought "would . . . be productive of much harm to the work"[1]; for it was a rebuttal of Coleridge's attack on *Bertram.* Scott had also objected to Maturin's first preface, on the ground that it would simply alert more people to the existence of Coleridge's ill-tempered tirade.[2] The version of the preface that Maturin did publish cannot be thought totally successful: its recounting of past failures certainly must have caused readers to scrutinize *Women* for evidence of continued failure.

The plot of *Women,* as the preface would lead us to expect, is indeed comparatively straightforward; but the novel opens misleadingly with a scene that smacks of Gothic sensationalism. Charles De Courcy, the orphan heir to property in southern Ireland, is on his way to Dublin to enter the university. Walking the last few miles because the stage had broken down, he is passed in the twilight by a racing carriage containing a screaming female and a man who is urging the driver to greater speed. De Courcy runs after the carriage but cannot keep sight of it. He enters a cottage kept by a mad crone, whose insane gesticulations urging him to leave make him aware of a door leading to another room. He forces himself past her and sees lying on the bed a beautiful young woman. After being enfeebled temporarily by the sight of her beauty, he carries away the insensible girl, despite the protests and imprecations of the crone, who falls into a paroxysm. De Courcy returns the girl to her guardian. The novel thereafter becomes a study of society and of the types of religious personalities; the only significant further appearances of Gothicism coincide with those of the mad crone.

As in *Fatal Revenge,* certain secret information in *Women* is not given until the last chapters; but only a most obtuse reader could miss the hints in *Women* about the "secrets." The mad crone is the young girl's maternal grandmother, who had wished to save the girl's soul by sending her to Catholic Spain. Years before, the crone had been the mistress of a dissolute Irishman who had thrown her out of his home when she had insisted that their daughter be reared as a Catholic. She lost her mind but not her devotion to her religion. Meanwhile, her lover hired Signore Dalmatiani, an Italian music-master, to tutor the daughter; and he, an opportunist, persuaded the fifteen-year-old girl to marry him secretly. When she was about to give birth to a child, the secret marriage was revealed to the girl's father. Enraged, the father expelled both his daughter and her husband. Her husband sent the newborn child to his father-in-law, told his wife that her baby had died at birth, and took her to Italy, where he forced her to earn their living on the stage. She became the most accomplished actress and singer in Europe.

Her father, not wishing the presence of his granddaughter Eva to restrain his debauchery, had given her to a woman of good repute who in time married a Mr. Wentworth. The Wentworths are fanatic Calvinists, and Eva has grown up to be a simple girl with a sympathetic heart but with little mental vigor. The grandfather finally writes to Madame Dalmatiani, his daughter, to tell her that her daughter had not died at birth. Now widowed, she comes to Dublin on the pretense of giving a farewell concert tour, while her father is deciding whether to reveal to her the name of her daughter—who is, of course, the female rescued by De Courcy.

Madame Zaira Dalmatiani is so youthful-looking that De Courcy thinks she is only twenty; and, though he had become engaged to Eva before he meets Zaira, he feels a strong attraction to this woman of the world. A good part of the first two volumes of the novel builds a contrast between the mother and daughter which centers on De Courcy's inability to choose decisively between them. (He is, of course, unaware that they are related.) These volumes justify a modern judgment that *Women* "is a study of inner life, a novel too advanced for its age, and a sensitive portrayal of young love."[3] Eva is immensely quiet, having no intellectual interests or social accomplishments; Zaira, the most intellectual woman in Europe, constantly amazes cultured groups by the authority with which she settles arguments by classical and contemporary literary allusions. Zaira is independent; Eva, dependent and clinging.

The outcome of the conflict within De Courcy is as much in doubt as his own real tastes. Before Zaira entered the scene, De Courcy is pleased that Eva's modesty and principles prevent her feeling earthly passion as he does. But he fears that their "perpetual conflict of opinions and habits was no happy prelude to domestic union"; and, after he has met Zaira, De Courcy finds the home of the Wentworths, which is the social hub of the Calvinists of Dublin, far too disputatious and narrow-minded for him. He hesitates temporarily, because during a fever the mental image of Eva remains as she herself is in life and is more appealing to him than that of Zaira, which becomes fantastic and evokes images of Hell. When he recovers and goes to visit Eva, there is a "glow of meeting"; but it fades away, and "Eva had not one ray of intellect to rekindle its lustre." Zaira, too, resists her love for De Courcy, trying to convince herself that she uses her intelligence to improve him for altruistic reasons. De Courcy and Zaira's affair is forced to an issue when the actress plans to return to Paris when her father dies suddenly, without having told her where her daughter is. De Courcy grovels at her feet and proposes; she accepts but refuses immediate marriage. She suggests they visit the Continent for a year posing as strangers. "She resolved, even in this exigency of her feelings, to try to develope his character; to enlarge his mind; and to fix his heart."

Zaira and De Courcy arrive in Paris in May, 1814, following the restoration of the Bourbons, a time of excitement and superficial emotions. De Courcy's head is turned almost immediately, and, being treated as an intellectual equal by Frenchmen, he does not take kindly to Zaira's ill-disguised efforts to train him in intellectual discourse by her own example. De Courcy cannot contest with her, and his sympathies—and shortly his affections—go from her to Mademoiselle de Touranges, whose feeble feminine remarks on Shakespeare are tartly corrected by Zaira. In rapid sequence, De Courcy learns that his intellectual friends pity him because they think he is trying to gain eminence by being the known favorite of an actress; that Zaira has had a husband and a child (whom she has never told him about); and that his guardian, Mr. Asgill, disapproves vehemently of his alliance with a woman who is both an actress (who is used to public display of her person) and a woman of literature (who is naturally crass and prideful).

As before with Eva, De Courcy vacillates—between marrying Zaira (so he cannot hurt anyone else) and returning to Ireland and Eva. The news that Eva is dying impels him to leave Paris, abandoning both Zaira and Mademoiselle de Touranges. But, when he arrives in Dublin, the Wentworths do not allow him to see Eva, partly to ease her last hours and partly because Mr. Wentworth wants to ensure that Eva's fortune will come to him rather than to a husband. Zaira, abandoned in Paris, is tempted to become an atheist; but she ultimately follows De Courcy to Dublin.

The climax is fully as crowded as that in *The Wild Irish Boy,* but Maturin is enough in control in *Women* to need no *deus ex machina.* By chance, Zaira learns that the mad crone, now dying, is her mother and that her "unknown" daughter is Eva Wentworth. She rushes to the Wentworth house; but Eva has expired peacefully minutes before Zaira throws herself on the sickbed. De Courcy dies in his sleep two days after Eva's funeral. He and Zaira—both stupefied by Eva's death—had merely looked at each other without interest at the funeral. Zaira continues to live in Ireland, but she does not sing any more. She says frequently, "My child—I have murdered my child!"

As with *The Milesian Chief,* the most regrettable thing about this novel is Maturin's presentation of its hero. De Courcy is early described as generous, brave, and sensible; but we quickly suspect that Maturin means "sensible" in the eighteenth-century sense of possessing sensibility; for, after his initial act of bravery in rescuing Eva from her abductors, he does nothing, says much, and *feels* tremulously. Still, the depiction of a credulous and irresolute sentimentalist contains a good deal of natural interest. We might object to De Courcy as a potential associate in real life, but he is consistently characterized and with considerable insight through the first two volumes and the first few pages of the third volume.

Then, suddenly, in the third volume the focus of narration shifts from De Courcy, where it had been located in the first two volumes—though from an omniscient point of view—to outside him, usually to Zaira and occasionally to one of her Parisian friends, Madame de Viosmenil. The effect of increased narrator distance is to make De Courcy a cold and callous man, while previously his flaws had been impetuousness and inability to modify his oscillations in emotions. His mental stature is deflated in Paris, where he is not as intelligent and promising as he had been in Ireland, despite his acceptance by the Parisian intellectuals; and he changes from being high-minded to being a petty discontent. He objects to Zaira's mental superiority though she displays it only to please him, and he feels that she treats him as if she were Catherine the Great and he one of her minions though they are living chastely apart and neither takes money from the other. Zaira had been quite correct in her assessment of him in Ireland: De Courcy needs wider experience and greater maturity before marrying.

It is not at all certain that Maturin's purpose in altering De Courcy's presentation, though, is to underline the accuracy of Zaira's analysis of the young man; nor does it seem to be to contrast the level of Irish and French conversation. (There are indeed slurs against Frenchmen's levity and their lack of morality; Zaira once thinks she should have taken De Courcy to Italy first, where he could have acquired a taste for reflection amid "the awful solitudes of antiquity.") Instead, the dilution of De Courcy's position in the novel seems to be the effect of Maturin's continuing inability to hold the reader in more than one orbit of interest at a time—an inability compensated for to some degree by the high quality of some of the vignettes which constitute such novels as *Fatal Revenge.* In *Women,* Maturin is dealing centrally with several characters; but he can maintain interest in only one at a time—first De Courcy, then Eva (in a less decided way), and then Zaira.

Moreover, competing with characters for central interest is Maturin's handling of religion, which develops into a kind of professional evaluation. The decline of De Courcy as a character and the increase in attention paid to Zaira seem to take place partly for this reason. Maturin takes immense pains with Zaira's temptations to take refuge in atheism and in suicide during her grief at De Courcy's return to Dublin. The section treating of her dilemma is so artificial and lengthy (just over a hundred pages) that it constitutes a digression, even though the effect on Zaira is immense. Walter Scott's objection to the length of the section is based on its redundance: "All these moods of a despairing mind are well described, but too much protracted. The mind becomes weary of accumulated horrors, having all reference to the same person and set of events, and belong to a catastrophe which is inevitable, and full in view."[4]

An atheist, de Cardonneau, slants his remarks to Zaira to suggest either that man's misery was determined for some indiscernible reason by God or that there is no God who has an authority to alleviate suffering. As if to underscore his qualifications to present such a religious debate in fiction, Maturin enters the novel in his own voice at this point—which, of course, takes us still further from the illusion that had been built up in the first two volumes. Maturin's view is that sufferers do not wish to ascribe their sufferings to an intelligent Cause, for an intelligent Cause cannot be thought to inflict sufferings without provocation, and thus suffering implies guilt; therefore, blind chance is more comforting.

Zaira is nearly convinced by de Cardonneau; but, coming across a wooden figure of Christ on a cross while walking in the woods on the night that she hears his argument, she falls on her knees and begs forgiveness. She then thinks of becoming a nun: "A complete exemplar of the annihilating effect of monasticism—torpid, obtuse, self-contracted, self-sufficed, without malevolence or kindness, pleasure or pain, love or grief." Zaira asks God if such is the requirement He makes of his chosen beings—that is, peace in exchange for life. She does not become a nun, but she does give up art, music, conversation; and, in fact, she approximates a monastic seclusion with her mourning for De Courcy's apostasy. The effect of de Cardonneau's efforts, then, has ironically been to turn her to a misanthropic religion. Her health is debilitated; and, because of the nervous strain she has undergone, her pride is destroyed so that she follows De Courcy abjectly to Ireland.

In this section, Maturin as the professional clergyman attacks demon atheists and the inhuman monasticism that typifies the Catholicism he loathed so deeply. De Cardonneau appears nowhere else in the novel and Maturin does not bother to motivate him in the least, and so his characterization is flat, and theatrical in the worst degree. The sequence as a whole is an impressive display of Maturin's knowledge of the psychology of religious conversion, but Zaira moves like a marionette from one carefully sketched state of mind to another.

The brunt of Maturin's attack on inadequate religions is felt by the Calvinists,[5] though his criticism of the Calvinists' narrowness in practices and social living is founded as much on individual failings as on standards of theology. Maturin stresses the Calvinists' interest in "points" that can be used to establish the certainty of the formulator's salvation, the sophistical interpretation of fine theological distinctions, and the doctrine that the gates of heaven are so carefully controlled that they open only to those who have command of the most minute elements of Scripture. He satirizes, through Mr. Wentworth, the Calvinists' hypocritical interest in wealth. Through the example of Macowen, one of the loudest members of the Wentworth group, Maturin implies the coxcombry of their preachers. Macowen is the son of a poor Irish peasant, educated because he caught the fancy of his landlord's evangelical wife, and now wishing to marry a wealthy evangelical woman. His choice had been Eva before De Courcy's wealth had attracted Mr. Wentworth's approval.

That the Calvinists lack the social polish that Maturin considered important is indicated, especially in the first volume, by their rude and insistent efforts to convert De Courcy. Indeed, one of Wentworth's reasons for allowing De Courcy to court Eva is his secret enjoyment of the prospect of controversy in trying to convert him. Maturin also attacks the Calvinists' essential heartlessness. Mr. Wentworth is elated into "a kind of splenetic good humour" when De Courcy breaks his engagement with Eva for the sake of Zaira; for he now has the opportunity for all manner of exhortations, strictures, and lamentations. Mr. Wentworth objects to a request that Eva makes on her deathbed, that she be allowed to die privately, without the other Evangelicals around. He thinks his ward owes him at least the material for an obituary article in an "Evangelical Magazine," on the assumption that in her last moments she would make an appropriately grandiose testament of faith. Eva rebukes him, saying that death is no ecstasy as the Evangelical Magazines had said, but an awful thing to a dying sinner.

But though Maturin pointedly satirizes Calvinism, the satire is relieved by indications that Maturin is attacking excesses and prejudices, not everything connected with the faith. Maturin wrote Scott that *Women* "will set the evangelical world in arms"; but, as Idman comments, the satire in *Women* "never has a ring of personal animosity; on the contrary, it is relieved by a tone of genuine humour."[6] The humor is most evident in the caricatures of Macowen and Wentworth; and the gloom and disputatious nature of Calvinism are partially offset by the moral superiority and humaneness of many Calvinists, such as De Courcy's kindly guardian Mr. Asgill. A young friend of De Courcy's, Montgomery, is a dedicated Calvinist but is more pertinently characterized by his suppressing his own love for Eva when he realizes that only De Courcy can make her happy; he even risks humiliation in challenging Zaira's ideas in public with the hope of luring her into committing blasphemy that will disenchant De Courcy with her and send him back to Eva. Mrs. Wentworth, one of the best-rounded characters in Maturin's novels, respects her husband but can barely restrain her impatience with his cant and intolerance; she feels pity for both Eva and De Courcy without sentimental excess in either instance. Eva, pure but ignorant, is a testament both to Calvinism's purifying influence and to its limitations; but, like Mrs. Wentworth, she is not merely a religious cipher but a characterization that has an existence separate from her religious context. Her unhappiness stems not only from her religious incompatibility with De Courcy; she lacks the personal forcefulness needed to keep De Courcy's love. She does not recognize the depth and intensity of her feelings for De Courcy, and in trying to constrain it to conventionally pallid forms she brings on her fatal illness, the inevitable end of which is only hastened by De Courcy's faithlessness. This idea of a fatal love is of course a sentimental cliché, but by basing it on a refusal to acknowledge physical passion instead of on heightened ethereality, Maturin gives it more substance than is contained in the usual death of a virtuous innocent.

Maturin himself comments, when De Courcy begins to criticize Wentworth's piety as a standard Calvinist failing, that De Courcy "indulged himself in the bad habit of transferring the censure due to individuals only, to the whole society." By suggesting that this same sort of transferring of censure can occur toward Catholics, Maturin tacitly modifies his strictures toward them in his works. Zaira remarks to an old dowager that "Catholics can be saved"; and she declares herself a nonsectarian Christian who has attended worship in "churches, chapels, and meeting-houses," in many of which she had heard "eloquence and genius; in all of them religion, as pure as we can expect to hear it from the lips of man." To the dowager's sarcastic retort that "it is a pity there is not a synagogue in Dublin," Zaira calmly says that it is indeed a pity there is not, for "it is a proof of the poverty of the city."

The language of *Women* is much more restrained than that of any of Maturin's previous writings,[7] giving the book an essentially orthodox kind of realism. One of the more successful portions of the book is De Courcy's courtship of Eva. The sheltered girl has heard only religious sentiments all of her life and is able to react only idealistically to her first kiss: "The first pledge of love was received by Charles with a feeling far different from that with which it was communicated; by him with the maddening enthusiasm of earthly passion; by her with the feeling of a seal to an eternal union." During a long prayer De Courcy's "burning glances" held an expression "so different from that of the feelings with which she was trying to fill her heart, and hoping to communicate to his, that it was in vain she attempted to shrink from a painful consciousness of their meaning." These scenes are not those of the lacey novel of manners, but represent the clash of breeding and disposition of two well-meaning individuals.

The prose style of *Women* is one that lends itself to witty turns of phrase as a natural part of the rhetoric. At a picnic outing, the selfish idlers of Dublin society are distressed at the approach of a storm. "It was ludicrous to hear the selfish expressions of regret, and something like reproach, as if Heaven was pledged for the happiness of the party." When Zaira realizes in Paris that De Courcy is chafing at his situation, "She clung like declining royalty to forms [of affection]."

Women is the most relaxed of Maturin's novels, the plot the simplest, the style the most cordial. The reason perhaps may be that Maturin felt the success of *Bertram* augured well for his future income; he wrote the novel before the one-day run of *Fredolfo* destroyed his hope of wealth from the stage. Certainly he felt more comfortable with the material of *Women* that he had with that of *The Wild Irish Boy,* for instance. *Women* is as rich in humor as it is in erudite allusion. Both qualities imply just cause for Maturin's own social popularity in Dublin at this time; and although the erudition was treated with scorn by some of the contemporary reviewers,[8] Maturin employed his learning with an ease and polish. The erudition inevitably "dates" the novel, since its allusiveness belongs to an age of Classical education; but the humor is still effective. It is not brilliant or incisive, but it is highly consonant with the general manner of *Women.* It is relaxed and unstrained, satirical but nonwounding. Its object is often the Calvinistic religion, but the tone is of reconciliation rather than of alienation, quite different from that of the searing criticisms of Catholicism in *Melmoth the Wanderer.*

CHAPTER 5

Melmoth the Wanderer:
The Form of Accomplishment

M *ELMOTH the Wanderer,* a marred masterpiece, mingles inconsistencies and bombast among splendidly realized passages of perversity and terror. The culmination of fifty years of Gothicism in England, it was written as much in response to recent Gothic productions like Mary Shelley's *Frankenstein,* John Polidori's *The Vampyre,* and especially Lord Byron's heroic dramas as in reply to the faked supernaturalism of Radcliffe and the grotesquely "genuine" supernaturalism of "Monk" Lewis. *Melmoth* measures up to the best qualities of preceding works: for Maturin uses atmosphere as effectively as Radcliffe, employs horrific scenes as grisly as anything in "Monk" Lewis' stories, and supports the narrative with as substantial an intellectual underpining as Godwin's *St. Leon* and *Caleb Williams* and Mary Shelley's *Frankenstein. Melmoth* is superior partly because Maturin arranged not to commit the infelicities inherent in these other writers' methods. For example, the protagonist Melmoth does, in fact, have powers more than human, so there is no need for the implausible ratiocination that brings three of Radcliffe's novels—and Maturin's *Fatal Revenge*—to their deflating conclusions; variety of subject circumvents the redundant horror that wearies the reader of Lewis; and a spontaneously keen, almost poetic relish in details of physical suffering makes *Melmoth* more realistic than *Frankenstein. Melmoth* also possesses a moral-esthetic superiority in the fineness with which the revelation of the self of the author is made to exhibit truths about human personality.

Maturin's frame of mind while composing this book can be deduced from the observations of a friend who often sat with him while he wrote it: "His mind travelling in the dark regions of romance, seemed altogether to have deserted his body, and left behind a mere physical organism; his long pale face acquired the appearance of a cast taken from the face of a dead body; and his

94

large prominent eyes took a glassy look; so that when, at that witching hour, he suddenly, without speaking, raised himself, and extended a thin and bony hand, to grasp the silver branch with which he lighted me down stairs, I have often started, and gazed on him as a spectral illusion of his own creation."[1]

It would be romantic to assume, as many commentators have done, that Maturin's spectral appearance is some sort of external evidence for the horrors he saw within mankind and which are reflected in the tortures and miseries experienced by Melmoth's victims in the novel. Part of his appearance, it is true, may be attributed to the effect upon his morbid genius of his awareness of man's potential for evil. Equally, though, his appearance was the result of privation, his parish work, demands for final payment of the debt he had become liable for, the harassment of his own creditors, and concern for his family. His wife presented him with a fourth child during the composition of *Melmoth;* and, including his seventy-four-year-old father, who had come to live with him, eleven people accustomed to genteel conditions were dependent upon him for subsistence. The distractions under which he existed probably contributed to the nervous energy which suffuses and inspirits *Melmoth,* but it also contributed to its sense of tenuous balance and spiritual chaos. A letter from the Constable firm indicates the dilemmas that Maturin's editors and printers confronted because Maturin's frantic activities caused him to forget to even number the pages of the manuscript:

We received by our Clerk a considerable quantity [of manuscript], but strange to say it was so unconnected, that with great difficulty, we found part of it belonging to the first Tale [presumably the "frame" story], and a part of it to the second [Stanton's tale], at least we thought so, so little however appeared to connect with the first Tale, that we could not make up the *third sheet* and what is just rec.d is in no way so far as we can notice, connected with what is received of the first tale—in one Word we are wholly at a stand, and it is utterly impossible that the work can proceed except some plan is pursued whereby the *connection* of the various portions of the MS. is kept up—there is no paging, no connecting words, nothing to guide us—and after corresponding for two months there are only two sheets set up and that without a title. . . . [2]

Despite this stern letter, which also includes a threat to stop the printing of the novel entirely, later letters indicate that Maturin continued to fail to answer queries from Constable (he delayed in offering a title, for example), but that he did send copy more rapidly than before. Even with the increased effort on his part, two full years elapsed between the date the book was contracted for and Maturin's final dispatch of manuscript: as Constable remarked, "a thing unheard of in Literary matters of this nature, we think."[3]

But, however distracted Maturin's mind may have been during the composition of the novel, *Melmoth* exerts a powerful effect. Eino Railo says of the mood of *Melmoth* that it is "almost impossible to ward off a certain oppressive and suffocating, nightmarish sensation, which increases the farther [one] reads. The world depicted is not the familiar one, but one envisaged in the light of a feverishly agonized mood, a world duskily-lit and stormy, behind it always an unknown, enigmatical, undefined terror, a force not to be measured or fought against with human weapons. The ruling atmosphere is a half-light reminiscent of Dante's *Inferno* and a paralyzing dread of some unknown, yet nearby terror."[4]

Railo attributes this sensation to the powerful characterization of Melmoth, a man who has sold his soul for knowledge and power, and whose presence ties together the individual tales that constitute the novel. Equally, or even more, influential is the brooding presence of the author, who senses oppressive forces everywhere trying to deprive mankind of its freedom and happiness, and who employs scenes of physical and mental torture to impart his sense of man's conscienceless assertion of his own wants over the needs of his fellows. His dwelling upon painful scenes with esthetic delight and with evident abandonment of conventional sympathy for others' agonies enforces an awareness of how close each man is to barbarity. In other words, the persona of the story is torn by conflicting positive and negative elements in his makeup. The "undefinable" terror that *Melmoth* instills rises in good measure from this reminder of the fearsome depths of instincts and potentialities that mankind would rather not acknowledge.

I   *The Devil, the Jew, and the Gothic Hero*

The strength of the novel derives in part from the utilization of European folklore. Melmoth's history and behavior endow him with the legendary qualities of Satan, Adam-Eve, Cain, Faust, and the Wandering Jew, in some contexts alternately but most frequently—and effectively—heterogeneously. Maturin draws upon both Goethe's and Marlowe's Faust. Maturin's protagonist, like Goethe's, seduces a virtuous female but is unable to persuade her to give up her soul; and Maturin's hero prepares for his end by warning away other humans on fear of forfeiting their lives in language taken directly from the end of Dr. Faustus.[5] The cause for Melmoth's damnation is also the same as Faust's: immensely curious and ruthless, he has mortgaged his immortal soul with the dark powers in exchange for knowledge of the universe's secrets and for freedom from the limitations of mortality for more than 150 years. Maturin combines the role of Faust with that of Mephistopheles, for Melmoth roams the earth offering surcease to people in misery and unbounded knowledge to the inquisitive on the terms that they must share his fate. Melmoth's questing for forbidden knowledge also links him to Adam and Eve, as his pride does to Satan, according to his own account: "Mine was the great angelic sin—pride and intellectual glorying! It was the first mortal sin—a boundless aspiration after forbidden knowledge!" Melmoth is also linked to Satan in another way; for like the devil in the Book of Job, Melmoth has only limited freedom. He cannot himself torture his intended victims, though he can help to ensnare them in the Inquisition by hinting to authorities that the victim is having converse with Satan or his agent (himself).

The Faustian overtones in Melmoth's existence are clearly the dominant ones; but just as interesting is the use Maturin makes of the legend of the Wandering Jew. The Wandering Jew is condemned to live an earthly life until the Second Coming of Christ. Different folk stories place different figures in this situation—Cain, Judas Iscariot, the Jew cured by Jesus of lameness but who refused Jesus' request to rest on his doorstep on the way to Golgotha, the man whose ear Simon Peter cut off in the Garden of Gethsemane, and a servant of Pontius Pilate who mocked Jesus for carrying the cross so slowly to his own crucifixion. The extent of Maturin's acquaintance with the literature of the Wandering Jew popular during his lifetime can only be surmised; but Melmoth displays characteristics shared by the Jew in most versions—most strikingly, his forceful burning eyes and his being accompanied by thunder (or, as in the case of Melmoth, by music). Like the *"ewigen Juden,"* Melmoth roves unceasingly. He cannot be harmed. Like the Jew in some versions, Melmoth is a bitter and sinister figure. Indeed, the despair and stubborn independence of the Jew in some versions make him quite clearly a prototype of the Gothic villain. The Wandering Jew recollects long-past events; Melmoth ingratiates himself on more than one occasion by an anecdotal history of Restoration dramatic and social personages.[6] Quite close to the Wandering Jew motif is the Rosicrucian legend of the man who knows the formula of the *elixir vitae* and who cannot die until he finds someone to whom he can give the secret. This legend, used by Godwin in *St. Leon,* is a clear precedent for the search-pattern plot of *Melmoth.*

The Faustian and Wandering Jew skeins blend so that a clear separation of tendencies is not possible, except that Melmoth's term of unusual life is strictly limited rather than potentially endless as is that of the Wandering Jew. Melmoth finds his immense learning and power joyless—a fitting state for a man who through an act of defiance of God learns how desirable subservience to God is. Like the Jew, rather than enjoying his powers, Melmoth spends all of his time in search of someone to share his fate—not out of loneliness, like Frankenstein's monster in desire of a mate, but out of bitter malignity.

While most of Melmoth's qualities derive from religious folklore, it appears that Maturin was directly energized in several of his tales by Polidori's *The Vampyre,* which appeared in 1819. This story of a monster who sucks the blood of his victims to sustain his own preternatural immortality is an analogue to the Faust-Mephistopheles and Wandering Jew legends, though its basis is in East European folklore. Several of the vampire's adventures, covered in a sentence or two in the brief story by Polidori, are turned into motifs or short tales by Maturin.[7]

The Gothic quality of *Melmoth the Wanderer,* especially in the earlier parts, is as pervasive as we would expect in the novel universally accepted as the greatest example of the genre. There are occasional references to Gothic architectural features; and, while there are no medieval castles, gloomy monastic buildings abound. Attacks upon Catholicism and monasticism dominate the early stories—the ones that are the least original and are even, in part, direct plagiarisms. The Gothicism is modified by Maturin's realistic bent and by a de-emphasis of certain Gothic conventions. For example, the Melmoth ancestral home, isolated and foreboding on the dark seacoast, is only a dilapidated Irish farm lodge.

The clearest derivative from Gothicism is of only peripheral importance. Each tale is accompanied by descriptions of the setting—invariably gloomy, with a flickering fire, dim candles, strong gusty winds outside, and dark wainscotting. The tellers are always intense, and they fearfully shoot glances into dark corners where the light either does not reach or creates impressions of lurking forms. The auditors, who always listen apprehensively, start abruptly at the slightest external sound. But, since nothing other than atmosphere depends upon the setting, Maturin seems to be utilizing the convention for mere effect. On one occasion, he sets the scene for a tale that is never told; on another, he describes the setting after the tale has been completed. Among other incidental Gothicisms that abound are a portrait whose eyes move, manuscripts long hidden in dark crevices, suggestions of necromancy, and incredible circumstances such as one protagonist's fleeing prison during a fire and falling exhausted on the tombstone of a brother killed in an earlier escape attempt.

Melmoth has most of the qualities associated with the Gothic hero-villain of the stage, an indication that Maturin took something of what he had learned while writing plays into the writing of novels. Ruthlessness, freedom from moral restraint, and indifference to others' pains make the central character appear villainous; courage, forcefulness, and agony make him appear sympathetic. His heroic qualities are partially negated by their lack of connection to human fears and limitations—once his quenchless curiosity has embroiled him in the irrevocable pact with Satan, his only human feelings are his love for Immalee and his shrinking from damnation. Melmoth himself is the only genuinely supernatural element in the novel; he remains in perpetual robust middle age, can transport himself rapidly from one distant point to another, and is immune from harm or death.

But his power has bounds, as I have already indicated. He causes none of the cataclysms associated with his presence, such as the shipwreck or the burning of the Inquisition prison. And his knowledge is limited to the range of his senses—he does not know that one of his intended victims has escaped the prison fire and is still alive. Maturin is devious on the matter of Melmoth's ability to command nature; for he implies that a lightning bolt which kills two lovers is of Melmoth's making. Moreover, a priest at whom Melmoth stares falls dead; and the teller of one tale about Melmoth dies minutes after leaving his auditor. But none of these deaths is explicitly attributed to Melmoth; indeed, the last two deaths are symbolic punishments for mediocrity. After their deaths, the priest and storyteller are revealed to have been men of unrestricted curiosity, but they have been incapable of equaling Melmoth's ultimate pursuit of the knowledge that they desire. Melmoth himself scoffs at the idea that he can control the weather and seas. As a result of the limitations on Melmoth's existence, most of the fear customarily created by the machinations of the villain of the Gothic novel is created in *Melmoth the Wanderer* not by the protagonist of the entire story but by the antagonists of the individual stories. But Melmoth's presence is an important moral element in our understanding of the novel: after the first story, the reader knows the terms that Melmoth will eventually offer the suffering characters.

Maturin, then, uses Gothic conventions with an instinct to their genuine but relative values. The most impressive effects of several of the stories are based upon realistic features rather than upon the artificial awesomeness of Melmoth or upon the obsessiveness of the Gothic frame of mind implicit in Melmoth's frantic search. The variety, as well as the consistency, of subject and handling prohibits glib classification of *Melmoth* as simply a genre novel. It *is* certainly a Gothic novel before it is anything else; but it is also a novel of ideas, a repository of personal philosophy and self-revelations, and a technical tour de force. None of these points needs to be forced, nor could it be without distorting the unity of the novel; but all of them need to be recognized.

II   *Story and Method*

Fortunately, *Melmoth the Wanderer* is still in print; for its six fully developed fictional situations employ more details than can be given here. The plot is not especially complex, nor is it difficult to follow,[8] but it consists of a series of generally brief stories, stories within stories, and stories within stories within stories—some written, some oral. During "The Tale of the Indies," a major part of the book, the narration is once thrice-removed from Maturin.

The explanation for this elaborate organization goes beyond esthetics to practicalities: Maturin's perpetual impoverishment. He realized he had conceived a scheme comparable to those of *Arabian Nights* and *Decameron*. With no limit to the number of victims Melmoth could torment, even before Maturin had half finished *Tales* (the working title), he was projecting a "continuation," with either Constable or Henry Colburn of London, who had offered him £500 for the second set of *Tales;* and that the novel was conceived of as a series of related but independent stories goes far to justify the discontinuity many readers of *Melmoth* feel.[9] Maturin ended the first set of *Tales* in a manner that would have permitted the resuscitation of Melmoth; but a second set was not written, probably because Maturin's health prevented his writing at all for two years, by which time he had arranged to write a historical novel for Constable.

The "frame" narrative deals with John Melmoth, a nineteenth-century descendant of the titular figure. Nothing of significance happens to the contemporary John Melmoth, although legend has it that the demonic Melmoth—also surnamed John—pursues the members of his family as assiduously as he does any stranger. John Melmoth the younger, the "collector" of all the Gothic tales that the novel contains, reads a moldy manuscript written by a seventeenth-century Englishman, John Stanton; and he listens to the strange story of Alonzo Monçada, who has been shipwrecked off Ireland's coast. Monçada, in turn, not only relates his own adventures in attempting to flee a monastic life, but he repeats stories told him by fellow monks and by a parricide who has been bribed to help him escape the monastery. Monçada also repeats verbatim a letter-narrative by his brother and an immensely long manuscript he has translated for a Jew while he was hiding from the Spanish Inquisition. And within this manuscript there is not only the long story involving the love between Immalee and the Wanderer, but two stories told to Immalee's father, one by Melmoth and one by the man who dies mysteriously after finishing his story.

The novel's ostensible unity is explained in the preface: the book is intended to illustrate a phrase from one of Maturin's own sermons—that despite the disobedience of man that has caused his fall from grace, there is not one person so unmindful of true value that he could sell his soul to the devil for "all that man could bestow, or earth afford." But the true unity of the book lies in the depiction of oppressive institutions—religious, social, and political —and their conflicts with individual inclination. Man strives individually to be good and loving and "Christian," but his institutions are repressive, sterile, and hypocritical. This theme is the real subject of *Melmoth*, and it is made the more complex by evidences that beneath even the individual's congeniality lies the potentiality for cruelty. Maturin saw institutional cruelty as developing from this hidden self, which was allowed to surface in the anonymity of bureaucracy.

III   *The Tales*

The Frame Story: Melmoth in Ireland (1816): Notified that his uncle is dying, John Melmoth, a student at Trinity College in Dublin, hastens to his bedside—partly, at least, because he is the old man's heir. The characterizations of the rural Irish retainers in the Melmoth family home are among the most rounded in the book. Superstitious and selfish, they enlarge the sense of foreboding inevitable on such occasions; but the initial grimness is dissipated by their simultaneous concern for appearances and by their small acts of kindness for the dying old Melmoth, whose wine cellars and coal bins they have broken into as a matter of course after years of niggardly treatment by their wealthy but miserly employer. Similar unpretentious realistic scenes toward the end of the novel reinforce the impression from this early chapter that Maturin was confident enough of his skill as a Gothicist to indulge his natural affection for the Irish peasantry and his interest in homely details of everyday life and character. What there are of these qualities in *The Milesian Chief* and *Women* provide some of the more attractive features of those novels; in *Melmoth*, this interest achieves its appropriate function of enhancing the depiction of human life, and this portrayal emphasizes by contrast the fantastic nature of the existence of Melmoth the Wanderer.

   Old Melmoth remains true to his manner of life in the face of death: he trembles for his soul, not in the least aware of the irony of his equally great fear that he will have to pay for a coffin. He is dying of fright, having spent the last years of his life anxiously trying to decipher a manuscript he has hidden in a closet in his bedroom. During the old man's last moments, young John twice sees stepping out of the closet a figure who resembles a portrait he had seen in the closet when he had earlier gone in search of wine for his uncle. Among his uncle's last words is the information that the original of the portrait, which was painted in 1646, is still alive. John himself had thought that the eyes of the portrait had followed his motions within the closet, and he is more than willing to carry out a request in his uncle's will to destroy the portrait and the manuscript.

But he first reads the manuscript (at midnight, of course), and it provides the first interpolated tale.

Tale of Stanton (1677): Stanton learns of Melmoth the Wanderer while traveling through Spain. Deserted one night by a cowardly guide, Stanton witnesses a terrifying incident. The bodies of two lovers killed by a bolt of lightning are approached by a calm stranger who bursts into "a laugh so loud, wild, and protracted, that the peasants, starting with as much horror at the sound as at that of the storm, hurried away." Finally finding lodging, despite Spanish loathing of the English, Stanton listens to an old woman's narration of a wedding disrupted by the appearance of the same stranger seen that night, before whose glare Father Olavida, a priest known for his sanctity, and secretly characterized by egoistic complacency in his reputation, had fallen dead.

Stanton is fatally fascinated by Melmoth's existence when he sees him again after a bawdy Restoration play in London; Melmoth tells him that they will meet again in a madhouse: "I *never desert my friends in misfortune. When they are plunged in the lowest abyss of human calamity, they are sure to be visited by me."* Previously known for singularity of behavior, Stanton is now suspected of insanity because of his constant talk of Melmoth. An unprincipled relative, Stanton's natural heir, arranges to trap Stanton in a madhouse, where he ultimately loses hope and allows himself to become as unkempt and loathsome as the other inmates. Melmoth appears according to his promise, and he makes Stanton a proposition that even in recollection agitates Stanton so much that the manuscript is illegible. Eventually freed, Stanton continues to seek Melmoth; and he leaves his manuscript at Melmoth's Irish home while on a journey there.

Two points about Stanton's story are of particular and immediate interest. Maturin introduces here the theme of madness, which appears in almost all of the stories. Some characters, such as Walberg in "Tale of Guzman's Family" and John Sandal in "The Lovers' Tale," actually become incapable of conducting their own lives; other characters are driven to the verge of insanity by Melmoth's machinations and by the persecutions of their fellow human beings. Alonzo Monçada, in particular, is affected by this motif: he is treated like a lunatic by his superiors when he tries to stolidly accept the regularity of monastic life; he oscillates maniacally between hope and despair while waiting to begin his escape from the monastery; after the attempt's failure, he feels like a "recovered maniac." His brother lapses into "partial insanity" in his eagerness to help Alonzo escape from the monastery. Other than serving as a thread to give the stories another element of internal unity, the theme of madness is important in that actual madness frees one from Melmoth's influence; for one must accept the choice that Melmoth offers with rational compliance. Stanton is not taken in by Melmoth's sophistical argument that he might be driven insane by living in the madhouse and lose his soul by committing blasphemy or a crime. The theme of madness, then, adds a level to the idea of moral responsibility; it also suggests another hindrance to Melmoth's ever achieving his goal.

The insanity actually present in the asylum itself bears directly upon Maturin's idea of merit. Little sympathy is shown to the inmates who have been driven mad by political ambitions frustrated by the Puritan Wars and the Restoration, by business failure, by amorousness, or by the kind of religious intensity which makes one weaver contemptuous of his fellows in the morning when he is certain he is one of the elect and a blasphemous wretch at night when he is certain he is one of the damned. But sympathy toward a woman who had lost all of her children and her husband in the Great Fire of London is shown by the silence enforced upon the other inmates by the "cry of nature" she utters in reliving the fire. "Terrifying as the out-break of her frenzy always was, Stanton used to await it as a kind of relief from the dissonant, melancholy, and ludicrous ravings of the others." (One may observe the similarity between this madwoman's dignified raving and that of the old hag of *Women* whose memories of her daughter Zaira are revived by the sight of a burning building.)

The time and place of Stanton's story permits Maturin to enlarge upon the literary genre he had been working in before writing *Melmoth,* the drama, and his favorite period of English history, the Restoration, to which he returns in greatly expanded context in "The Lovers' Tale." Maturin describes the conditions of dramatic performance, the box audience composed of lovers and men of wit, the critics in the pit "armed cap-a-pee [*sic*] from Aristotle and Bossu." He makes an observation whose truth he did not benefit from in his own stage-writing: "Vice is always nearly on an average: The only difference in life worth tracing, is that of manners." The sense of genuineness in the novel is greatly enhanced by this and other historical "digressions" by Maturin, such as those in "The Lovers' Tale." These passages of historical sketching, along with the frank literalness of the Irishness in the frame story, remind us again that the "wellsprings of fearful thought" was not Maturin's sole true subject.

The night after young John Melmoth burns the portrait and Stanton's manuscript, a ferocious storm, reminiscent of the one in *Bertram,* wrecks a ship on the coast off Melmoth's estate. Maturin justifies in orthodox Gothic terms his use of Radcliffean atmosphere: "Terror is very fond of associations: we love to connect the agitation of the elements with the agitated life of man." The Irish servants fearlessly brave the furious winds to see if anyone can be saved, but Maturin's praise of them is restrained by his observation that a good part of their courage comes from their complacency about their own safety. There is only one survivor from the ship, Alonzo Monçada, the son of a Spanish duke. Monçada saves not only himself, but young Melmoth, who had fallen into the sea from a precipice in pursuit of a figure (the Wanderer) who had sternly watched the ship in distress, who was as unmoved by the storm as by the spectacle, and whose laugh chilled young Melmoth's blood. When Monçada learns that he is in the house of Melmoth's descendant, several days are required for his agitations to cease long enough for him to tell his story, which constitutes the remainder of *Melmoth,* apart from occasional remarks and the final catastrophe.

The Tale of the Spaniard (ca. 1800): Monçada is illegitimate, his father's love for a girl of inferior rank having been opposed by the previous duke until after Alonzo's birth. To atone for her guilt, his mother had promised to God that her unborn child would become his minister. Monçada has no inclination to the monastic life, but his appeals are twice borne down by his mother throwing herself at his feet to implore that he not make her weakness known to the world by refusing the cowl, nor commit injustice against his legitimate younger brother, the acknowledged heir.

Life in monasteries is, as we have observed, a favorite topic of Gothic fiction, and nowhere is it more markedly portrayed than in *Melmoth.* The typical depiction of monasticism in English Gothic novels is as a hotbed of perversion, cruelty, satanism, and political intrigue. *The Monk* of Lewis spawned no end of formless diatribes against Catholic practices, but Maturin's loathing for monasticism is more ingrained than that of any other Gothic writer. The immediate impetus for his *Five Sermons of the Errors of the Roman Catholic Church* was the conversion of a wealthy Dublin woman who thought of sealing "her conversion by embracing the dreary and heartless profession of conventual celibacy."[10] Maturin's hatred encourages his bent for vivid detail of persecution and setting, but the exaggeration inherent in Gothic conventions is muted by the soundness of Maturin's psychological preparation for the heinous indifference to suffering that he sees as inevitable in a monastic existence. Whether or not life in a monastery conformed to Maturin's portrayal of it,[11] the portrayal itself is based on a uniform concept of human nature. There is essential truth to nature in Lewis' Ambrosius, who is turned from stern piety to conscienceless lust by confinement in a celibate society;[12] but the extremes to which Ambrosius' lust drives him weaken the effect of *The Monk* by their exoticism. Maturin avoids distortion by broadening the base of monkish motivation; he stresses not sexlessness but the absence of all normal human concerns. "Monastic life [is] like the wrong side of tapestry."

Bereft of normal outlets for energy and interests, Maturin's monks turn not to satanism, as did Ambrosius, but to gossip about everyone else's slightest activity, to petty malignity, and only finally to cruelty and intrigues. Initially delighted that the Duke of Monçada's son has joined their order, they quickly resent the aloofness by which Alonzo hopes to dull the senses that can never enjoy the attractions of the outside world, interpreting his behavior as a reproach to their own busy but trivial ways of passing their time.

Monçada's natural revulsion toward conventual life is given further substance when a young monk who had offered unauthorized kindness to a sufferer undergoing penance is punished so severely that he dies. Then a dying monk noted in the monastery for sanctity disillusions Monçada of his remaining idealism by proclaiming the deadening effect of the unnaturalness of the regimen —praying when a bell rings, eating when a bell rings, rising from a bed to say matins before one has fully rested. The monk expresses total lack of religious belief, describing the "inevitable" religious progression from faith to doubt, and concluding that his only feeling at facing death is relief that his wretched life has come to a close.

Despising the convent's barren rigidity of form, Monçada rushes from the bedside of the dead monk into the garden, where he feels disposed to pray for the first time: "The garden, with its calm moonlight beauty, its innocence of heaven, its theology of the stars, was at once a reproach and a consolation to me." At this point in his revulsion, Monçada is offered hope. His brother had just heard of the emotional coercion that had forced Alonzo to become a monk. Chivalrously angered, the younger Monçada resolves to free his brother from the convent.

The brother's first effort is through legal means, based on the claim that the vow had been extorted from Alonzo. This plan fails; for, though the tribunal recognizes the truth of the claim, it fears that every monk in Madrid would be demanding his freedom if Alonzo is allowed to go free. The time leading up to the trial is one of the more interesting and better-paced sections of the novel, although composed of normal events for a Gothic novel.[13] The Superior of the monastery, dedicated to the ideal of monastic discipline, permits the other monks to try to induce Alonzo to withdraw his request to be released from his vows. He is placed for days in a dark dungeon infested with reptiles, deprived of all of the books and furniture in his cell, awakened at night by screams to see ghastly figures writhing in the air of his cell, and whispered to by disembodied voices that suggest indecencies concerning the Virgin Mary. Alonzo bears up well, recognizing that phosphorous paint on the

walls is responsible for the writhing figures; but the licentious suggestions whispered to the innocent boy keep him sleepless. He is
close to committing blasphemy in his weariness and terror, which
would lead to his being turned over to the Inquisition, when the
bishop of the area hears rumors of strange activities in the monastery and pays a visit. Horrified at Alonzo's condition, he commands that everything taken from him be returned and that he be
allowed to rejoin the other monks in religious worship.

After the legal effort has been frustrated, Alonzo's brother plots
an escape. He bribes a lay member of the monastic community
to conduct Alonzo through subterranean passageways to the
garden where they can climb over the wall in the dead of night.
The guide is a parricide who had evaded legal punishment by becoming connected to the monastery. But Alonzo has no choice,
and his fears are increased when the parricide tells how he had
murdered his father and two miscreant monks. Monçada's fore-
bodings are well founded. As soon as the two clamber over the
monastery wall, the parricide kills Monçada's waiting brother; and,
when Monçada awakens from the shock, he is a prisoner of the
Inquisition.

It is here, finally, that Melmoth the Wanderer enters "The Tale
of the Spaniard." Monçada is visited in the prison by a man he
takes to be an investigator for the Inquisition, though he arrives at
unusual hours and is never brought to Monçada's cell by a guard.
The Inquisition's suspicions are aroused by reports of strange conversations being heard from outside Monçada's cell. But Monçada
persists in thinking that the stranger's appearances are part of
the Inquisition's plot to trap him into a false statement. So he tells
all to the Inquisition, including the man's awful proposition that he
can have his freedom in exchange for his soul. Instead of granting
sympathy for his honesty, the Inquisition sentences Monçada to
be burned alive for having converse with the Devil.

As is almost always the case in the stories in which Melmoth
plays a subordinate role, his appearance in the Inquisition prison
decreases narrative tension. His temptation of Monçada follows
the more engrossing, if highly wrought, mental torture Monçada
has been put through by the perverted ecclesiastics. And the reader
already suspects from Maturin's preface that no one will ever
accept Melmoth's offer. The only point of interest remaining is

how Monçada will escape the auto-da-fé. The escape is handled in a manner similar to that of the protagonist of Godwin's *St. Leon,* and it is even more clearly similar to the coincidental revulsions of nature in *Fatal Revenge* that created earthquakes and floods to free characters from constrained situations. A fire breaks out in the prison; the Inquisitors place the prisoners in an open area; and, when a part of the stonework falls, Monçada rushes through.

He takes refuge in the home of a Jew who has supposedly become Catholic. Mutual terror acts as a common bond between the condemned ex-monk and the apostate Jew-Catholic; Monçada is given asylum.

He remains undetected until one day during a Catholic procession he stands too close to the window in fascinated horror as the mob recognizes the parricide taking part in the procession and rips him to pieces: "I echoed the wild shouts of the multitude with a kind of savage instinct." Monçada attracts the attention of Melmoth, who is taking part in the murder of the parricide; and the next day officers come to search the house. Put by the Jew through a secret trap door, Monçada rushes along a dark way until he comes upon a room containing skeletons in coffins who in life had been the family of the inmate of the room, the incredibly aged Jew, Adonijah. Adonijah has been a seeker after mysterious knowledge as had been Melmoth, and Adonijah has been cursed as a punishment to live a longer life than natural. (This punishment is, of course, ironic in the context of the novel, since the price Melmoth had extracted in exchange for his own soul was increased life.) Among the skeletons are those of people who had resisted Melmoth's temptation. Adonijah puts Monçada to work translating a long account of Melmoth's activities, which include the next three stories. Promised stories about the skeletons are never given; perhaps Maturin was holding this device for numerous stories for the projected second set of *Tales.*

"The Tale of the Spaniard" is intensely written. Maturin's animus against repression of individuality by institutions denying normal life activities gives to the scenes relating Monçada's tortures by the ex-Jesuit community[14] a quality of sustained anger that elevates them above the usual Gothic stress upon the unnatural bestiality of life under Catholicism. The Superior and the dedicated Inquisitors put public reaction, conventual discipline, and stereotypical interpretation of a man's words above individual considerations. Not surprisingly, many of the favorably portrayed Catholics are at heart Anglicans. The bishop who relieves Monçada from the excesses of the monastery's methods of persuasion is a "marble statue of Episcopacy, chiselled out by the hand of Catholicism"; even other Catholics suspect him of being liberal—that is, inclined to Protestantism. The reflections of Monçada himself are those of a Protestant clergyman musing on the conditions of life and their religious aspects: "Churchmen cannot bear to hear prayers uttered in a form different from their own. The cry of a solitary individual to God, sounds like profanation in their ears . . . . Alas! is it forms then that God regards? or is it not rather the prayer of the heart which alone reaches him, and prospers in its petition?"

Not all of Monçada's musings are strictly Anglican, for he never explicitly surrenders his Catholic faith. Many of his musings are simply sermonlike applications of generalizations to specific circumstances: afraid to mention to his guide his fear of not finding their way out of the subterranean passageway, Monçada thinks: "Perhaps the condemned spirits will feel thus at their final sentence, when they know all that is to be suffered, and dare not disclose to each other that horrible truth which is no longer a secret, but which the profound silence of their despair would seem to make one." Overall, Alonzo serves as Maturin's mouthpiece to express some his own values; and the parallels he draws between religion and life implicitly underline the negativeness of monastic isolation.

The Tale of the Parricide (ca. 1796): In the course of "The Tale of the Spaniard" occurs a narrative that is quintessentially Maturin —the story told by the parricide guide to Monçada in the nearly lightless subterranean depths of the monastery. Despite the absence of Melmoth, this brief section crystallizes the novel's major qualities—Gothic dankness, corruptive monasticism, commonsense rejection of idealization, brilliant evocation of suffering.

Maturin capitalizes upon the instinctive fear of dark places; he declares that Gothic romances are inadequate to relate the horrors of subterranean passages. On the journey through the monastery's tunnel, Monçada recalls superstitions of monks being deluded into the vaults of the institution and being forced to participate in a Black Mass—eating rotting flesh, drinking "the dead corrupted blood," and hearing the anthems of demons "on that awful verge where life and eternity mingle."

Nothing untoward actually is present in the brief journey except for the darkness and the close atmosphere; Monçada is susceptible to suggestions of horrible contingencies entirely of his own creation. He feels terror so strongly he thinks he could "feed on a parent, to gnaw out our passage into life and liberty"—a striking prelude for the tale which the parricide shortly tells. Detailing Monçada's fears creates an effective tone. Maturin does not inform the reader until later that the parricide guide had been along this way before, and even has had a map all during the present fearful trip. The power in this section, even after many readings, suggests two levels of horror: oppression by the unjust spiritual means that have brought Alonzo to being willing to risk the passageway, and innate superstitiousness and archetypal longings and loathings. The fear of being caught plays no part in Monçada's terror, although it increases suspense for the reader.

While waiting until dark before climbing through the trapdoor into the garden, Alonzo learns about his guide's character and the extent to which monasticism can modify moral principles. The parricide had been welcomed into the monastic community with the assurance that his powers would find plenty of employment there. One of his first tasks had been to rid the monastery of a monk and a novice, the latter being a woman who had surreptitiously joined the monastery in order to be near her husband. Pretending to help them flee, the parricide had guided them through the passageway that he and Alonzo had just come through and had locked them in a chamber where they had starved to death. He had been set there to watch their last agonies by the Superior in order to teach him "callosity of heart."

The step-by-step description of the victims' reaction to hunger is too long to quote in full. It is marked by progressive antagonism. The horror of detailed starvation is climaxed by desperate cannibalism. "In the agonies of their famished sickness they loathed each other—they could have cursed each other, if they had had breath to curse. It was on the fourth night that I heard the shriek of the wretched female,—her lover, in the agony of hunger, had fastened his teeth in her shoulder;—that bosom on which he had so often luxuriated, became a meal to him now." After the pair

are dead, the parricide draws back their cowls and discovers that
the wife had been his only sister. The basic idea of the story, monastic punishment by starvation in a dungeon, comes from the story
of Agnes in *The Monk*. Also in *The Monk,* Ambrosius rapes and
kills his sister Antonia while ignorant of the relationship. It is worth
pointing out, again, that Maturin borrows from the Gothic tradition and shapes his borrowings into new contours less grotesque
and more horrifying than the original sources possess. During all
of the adventures underground, there have been no gratuitous
supernatural thrusts by Maturin. He has relied upon Monçada's
imagination, and upon human corruption and limitations under
suffering, to create emotions which other Gothic novelists use
grosser methods to achieve.

The lover's cannibalism in entombment is the high-mark of the
novel's horror; but close upon the scene of cannibalism there are
other evocative descriptions that bear quotation. The description
of the death of the parricide can be fruitfully compared to that
of the prioress in Lewis' *The Monk* to illustrate the superiority of
hard detail to a general gloss in creating horror. Maturin borrowed
the incident from Lewis, but improved upon it. Lewis describes
the mob's action thus: "They refused to listen to her [pleas for
mercy]: they shewed her every sort of insult, loaded her with mud
and filth, and called her by the most opprobrious appellations.
. . . She sank upon the ground bathed in blood, and in a few minutes
terminated her miserable existence." This passage shows the end
of Maturin's parricide, as described by Monçada:

I saw, I felt, but I cannot describe, the last moments of this horrible scene.
Dragged from the mud and stones, they dashed a mangled lump of flesh
right against the door of the house where I was. With his tongue hanging
from his lacerated mouth, like that of a baited bull; with one eye torn from
the socket, and dangling on his bloody cheek; with a fracture in every limb,
and a wound for every pore, he still howled for "life—life—life—mercy!"
till a stone, aimed by some pitying hand, struck him down. He fell, trodden
in one moment into sanguine and discoloured mud by a thousand feet.

Another passage of gruesome detail is Monçada's dream, while
in the prison of the Inquisition, of being burned alive. Although
it is not Maturin speaking in his own voice, its obsessive and
intense introspection justifies a reference to it as "one of those

depictions of horror which point to a streak of perversity in his [Maturin's] mind"[15]:

My feet were scorched to a cinder,—my muscles cracked, my blood and marrow hissed, my flesh consumed like shrinking leather,—the bones of my legs hung two black withering and moveless sticks in the ascending blaze;—it ascended, caught my hair,—I was crowned with fire,—my head was a ball of molten metal, my eyes flashed and melted in their sockets:—I opened my mouth, it drank fire,—I closed it, the fire was within,—and still the bells rung on. . . .

The parricide employs an elevated ecclesiastical language and syntax in a manner similar to Monçada—evidence of Maturin's lack of attention to keeping his narrators distinct and also of his carelessness as to who should be clearly his spokesman. Outraged reviewers felt that Maturin was inuring minds to evil in having the despicable parricide speaking both blasphemous and sensible ideas.[16] The parricide observes that the foolishness of the idealism of the monk and novice's devotion to each other was laid bare in their death chamber: "A trivial and ordinary want [hunger], whose claims at another time they would have regarded as a vulgar interruption of their spiritualised intercourse, not only, by its natural operation, sundered it for ever, but, before it ceased, converted that intercourse into a source of torment and hostility inconceivable, except among cannibals." He even draws a relevant moral between himself and Monçada: "You killed [his parents, by refusing to become a monk] by inches,—I murdered [his father] at a blow,—which of us is the [greater] murderer?"

Despite the wisdom and common-sense deflation of idealism of some of the parricide's comments, he is essentially another means to excoriate monasticism's perverseness. He has seen too much hypocrisy and obsessive careerism in the short time he has been in the Church to take its tenets seriously; but, not wanting to take any chances on futurity, he has fostered Alonzo's pain in order to lessen his own eternal punishment. His is a sadistic, crudely inverted eye-for-eye theology which Maturin implies is only the natural construct from an observation of monastic practice.

The Tale of the Indians (1676): The plot of this section, the longest one in the novel, can be stated quite succinctly. Melmoth discovers on an island off the coast of India a European girl, who, having lived her entire conscious life in a state of nature, is totally virtuous. He reluctantly falls in love with her and finally marries her after she returns to her family in Spain. But, when she is brought under the Inquisition because her husband is recognized as the terrible Wanderer, he offers to her the same choice he has offered to Stanton and to Monçada.

Maturin organizes this tale by shifts in the setting and in Melmoth's motivations. Immalee's story has nearly equally interesting portions taking place on the isle in the Indian Ocean and in her parents' home in Spain—a shift that permits a great contrast in the satire on religious abuses. In the island setting, Immalee sees on the mainland, through a telescope that Melmoth furnishes, the various barbaric practices of the Juggernaut, Maha-deva, and Moslem religions—infant sacrifice, ritual suicide-murder of aged parents, and phallic worship. Maturin exploits every opportunity for gore, as in his description of emaciated Juggernaut pilgrims being devoured alive by vultures. One of Maturin's best critics finds ridiculous the attack upon loathsome practices of non-European religions, "which no one would have dreamt of defending."[17] But Maturin's point is that the Indian religions amplify the abuses of religions in Europe, just as his descriptions of European religions intensify the repression, guilt, and obedience that may be found in the world outside the stifling walls of a monastery.

Maturin's satire on religion in Spain takes the form of a basically good-humored attack upon family confessors who play too great a part in family decisions. The Aliaga family confessor, Fra Jose, is gluttonous and lazy but kind; his wit is attractively cutting rather than cruel. But, like the confessor of the Monçada family who is largely responsible for not letting Alonzo's mother neglect her promise to make Alonzo a monk, Fra Jose jealously relishes the power he wields over "his" family. It is the "system, not the individual, that we must blame." A concomitant contrast, based on the tale's two settings, is between the natural, active, invigorating life of Immalee on her isle, and the dull, formal, and witheringly monotonous Aliaga life as dominated by Catholicism.

The second kind of shift involves the various alterations of Melmoth's attitude toward Immalee (called "Isidora" in Spain). He twice renounces any further temptation of her: on the island, because she resists him even with Satan himself urging Melmoth on; in Spain, because he feels pity for her and vanishes "for ever" rather than allow her selfless love to damn her own soul. The effect of this second kind of shift is complicated by the suspense as to whether some one like Immalee might in her naïve innocence lose her soul in agreeing to a condition she would not fully comprehend. Of course, we can never expect strict consistency in a Gothic novel. In *Melmoth,* as in the dramas, Maturin plays often for an immediate transitory thrill. A frequent implication is that if Immalee agrees to join Melmoth "for ever," she will be damned even though Melmoth has not made clear the nature of his existence. She always draws back, as if the purity of her prereligious state keeps her from acceding to this proposal.

While she is on the island, she wants her wedding to take place in (symbolic) moonlight, a condition that Melmoth himself cannot abide. In Spain, the wedding takes place in the novel's most purely Gothic scene, which effectively contrasts Isidora's expectation of a life of luxury and comfort as an Aliaga and her coming life of misery and fear as Melmoth's wife. On a bleak night Melmoth leads her through a dark, steep path to an abandoned monastery where a sainted hermit lives. Unknown to Isidora, the hermit had died the night before; so she does not know the reason why the hand which joins hers and Melmoth's together in the pitch dark is "as *cold as that of death.*"

But she is not damned by this stealthy marriage to Melmoth, despite all of his previous statements to her that she will be with him "for ever" if she agrees to marry him; and the implication is that the decision to join Melmoth in his damnation must be a conscious one. When she agrees to marry Melmoth, she does it without conditions; Melmoth marries her out of sympathy for her being forced to consent to marry her father's choice, a merchant she has never met: "This union, in the same slight and tender form, of all those eternal competitors, energy and fragility, beauty and death, made every human pulse in Melmoth's frame beat with a throbbing unknown before." In the scene where they agree to marry, there are no references to his blasted state. In previous scenes, yes; but the agreement itself is neutral and thus does not ensure damnation. In the prison of the Inquisition, when Isidora is approached by Melmoth and told all the terms, she rejects him.

That the choice must be conscious and meaningful has already proved a relevant matter in Stanton's story. Furthermore, this aspect of the choice helps to resolve the problem raised by countless readers as to why Melmoth wastes immense energy on essentially virtuous people. Why, they ask, does he not offer his proposal to criminals? The parricide, who is "beyond the redemption of a Savior," should leap at the chance for earthly power.[18] Maturin's own position on this religious issue is that sin by emotion is only veniel, not mortal. What deserves eternal damnation is an intellectual violation of moral order and decency. To spend time with parricides and other criminals would not only be a waste of Melmoth's time; it would not serve Maturin's theological-pedagogical purpose of implying the dignity of his religious position and of showing the importance of both faith and works.[19]

It is important to realize that Melmoth has none of the sexual sado-masochistic bias usual to the Gothic villain. The point is explicitly made that he has never been devoted to sensuality. Maturin is not prudish, as the descriptions of sexual misbehavior in his society novels make clear; but his purpose in *Melmoth* simply makes sexuality irrelevant. Melmoth has all knowledge, and it makes him totally cynical and despairing. The attraction of Immalee for him is the possibility that her innocence might assuage the bitterness of contemplating his destiny.

This un-Gothic lack of physicality affects the entire novel. As a contrast to the gross sensuality of *The Monk,* where a detailed seduction, a rape, and two attempted rapes are given within the narrative, in *Melmoth* there is only one persecuted maiden, Immalee, and that maiden is married before she has sexual relations with her persecutor. All of Immalee's persecution by Melmoth, including the possibility of her bearing an illegitimate child because of Melmoth's refusal to publicly acknowledge the marriage, is narrated with no effort at licentiousness, possibly because the horror at the father's identity is stronger than the social shame of illegitimacy, which can be hidden by her wealthy family. Even the monk and the novice killed by the parricide are married, and their physical relationship contrasts with unnatural conventual repression.

Only in this tale is Melmoth's suffering human and sympathetic. There is a great deal of his usual fustian, but in the context of his being unable to share human happiness or to forget for long his damnation the fustian often has dignity. Maturin catches the essence of the Gothic villain's mingled agony and pride for his damned state that forbids normal human happiness:

"Poor girl," he exclaimed, with that mixture of bitterness and commiseration, that at once terrifies and humiliates: "and is this the destiny I am to fulfill?—to listen to the chirping of birds, and watch the opening of buds? . . . Tell me," he added with still wilder fierceness, "tell me from what line of my features,—from what accent of my voice,—from what sentiment of my discourse, have you extracted the foundation of a hope that insults me with the view of felicity?"

Idman sees, as the pattern of Melmoth's frustration, that "what causes him his keenest sufferings is not that he is shut out of paradise but that he is shut out of the community of the good among human beings." Melmoth is thus connected to the heroes of Byron and to the protagonists of Romantic literature in general. Idman's reading is amplified by Axton: "Melmoth's despair prompts the bargain he offers those brought to the verge of his own insane desperation by corrupt humanity. The bargain itself is their renunciation of belief in any ultimate moral order, their acceptance of the despairing madness which is Melmoth's torment and damnation. The relief the Wanderer seeks is the conquest of his hopelessness; and Immalee's essentially Christian love comes close to redeeming him."[20]

A highly charged scene on the island charts Melmoth's dilemma keenly. He tries to resist the unseen urgings of Satan himself—"This hour is mine, not thine"—and to treat Immalee with "mercy." But he finally forces the issue, asking Immalee whether she will marry him in the lurid lightning of a thrashing storm, similar to those scenes they must endure forever, "amid fire and darkness—amid hatred and despair." "Earth and heaven, the sea and the dry land, seemed mingling together, and about to replunge into chaos. . . . There was a fearful inversion of the natural appearance of earth and sea, as if all the barriers of nature were broken, and all her laws reversed." The scene uses nature in a superior Radcliffean manner as "an involuntary interpreter between us and our feelings," as Maturin expresses it just before the description of the storm quoted above.[21]

But "The Tale of the Indians" is, nevertheless, the least satis-factory of the novel's stories.[22] It is the only story in the novel in which Melmoth is himself a major actor, and the great difficulty in combining in one figure the legendary qualities of Faustus and Mephistopheles becomes apparent. In the early stories, though he was a frustrated Mephistopheles, his lack of sympathy for mere physical suffering and fear lends an aura of great superiority to his being. But in this tale, where he has the greatest degree of human intercourse, only a few of his speeches amplify our sense of his superhuman flawedness. Mephistopheles essentially vanishes; an agonized Faustus remains—and he is variously petty, terrorizing, despairing, sentimentally affected by Isidora's goodness and in-nocence, cruel, and vindictive.

But the inevitable limitations of language in fiction usually make the Melmoth of this tale not the awe-inspiring agent of Satan but a misanthropist and an often flat Gothic villain. The worn sophis-tical argument and tired diction of "Did you never trace a worm in the flower?" hardly impress us with Melmoth's satanic authority and devious scheming; nor does his remark that crushing flowers "is my vocation." His condemnations of worldly activities are on the level of the fulminations of a malcontent, as when he says that *all* kings and heroes are in hell. He is a more imposing figure in the Stanton and Monçada stories than he ever is after them. Once the reader has seen the ineffectiveness of his exertions—*these* two characters resist him—the superstitious feelings surrounding his appearances slacken. (As if recognizing this effect, in the last two tales of his novel Maturin has Melmoth's appearances given in reports by characters rather than in the narrative proper.) Also, Maturin continually is saying that Melmoth is torn by human feeling toward Immalee-Isidora; this conflict within him creates sympathy for Melmoth, but it becomes stale as a rhetorical device.

The more serious weakness in "The Tale of the Indians" comes about from Maturin's use of the Noble Savage theory. It results in the dual employment of two unrealistic and artificial conven-tions, Gothicism and primitivism, in one context. The rest of the novel's stories rely upon the contrast between realistic characters and situations, and the frightfulness of Melmoth's supernatural damnation. Immalee-Isidora develops toward wisdom and the recognition of pain, but her growth is peculiarly directionless.

She shows no real distress or even curiosity at the death of her servant on her wedding night; and she seems not to have ever asked Melmoth about his religious beliefs until she is committed to marry him. She never becomes real in the way that Zaira does in *Women;* too much of her ideality remains. Immalee always draws back instinctively whenever the risk of losing orthodox sympathy is encountered; her "unimaginable purity" protects her from understanding "the outrageous lubricities of the Phallic worship" that she observes through Melmoth's telescope. Zaira, on the contrary, while she never loses her chastity, loses the reputation for it in going to Paris with De Courcy, and she accepts the loss without lamentation.

There is also, in Immalee's delineation, an illogicality not fully accounted for by the conventions of the Noble Savage.[23] She was shipwrecked on the island when she was old enough to have learned Spanish, and her nurse survived with her for some time. Still, she does not realize that she is human and she even sees no similarity between herself and other human beings whom she sees, such as Melmoth and the occasional mainland visitor to the island, though she has seen her own image in water. She thinks of Melmoth as a *"new flower that had grown in the sand."* The animals around her on the island show a natural fear of thunderstorms; yet, she is shown again and again to be fearless of storms and human intruders because she is "ignorant" and "innocent."

The grossest violation of plausibility—and of the tenet of Noble Savagery that civilization is an educative if corruptive influence— appears toward the end of the story. After a year and a half in a deeply Catholic household that has a resident priest-confessor, Immalee-Isidora does not understand what Melmoth refers to when he talks of the "fires of hell." Her personality has a sentimental bent: she tells Melmoth she is glad that he has come to make her think and that she can "have the joy of tears" at Melmoth's absence. We should observe again that such implausibilities are customary in sentimental fiction; but in the other stories in *Melmoth* character development is realistic and causative—even the personality of Stanton, whose learning experiences are so stark. In the context of the entire novel, Immalee strikes a grossly false note that the attractiveness of her innocence and sentiments do not palliate.

Within the story about Immalee-Isidora, two stories concerning

Melmoth are told to Isidora's father during a long business trip through Spain. The first tale is told by a man who, like Stanton and Adonijah, has been collecting information about Melmoth; the second, by Melmoth himself. The justification for interjecting the stories within the context of Isidora's danger is that both are "warnings" for Don Francisco di Aliaga to return home and save his daughter. That Melmoth tells one of them is an interesting, though overdrawn, illustration of his ambivalence toward dooming the one whom he loves. The stories do not prevent the marriage, since Francisco continues dull-wittedly on his business way, taking little concern from the inexplicable death of the first storyteller shortly after he had finished his story, and not apprehending even Melmoth's explicit statement after the second story that his daughter is in great danger.

The Tale of Guzman's Family (pre-1676): More a domestic story than a horror story, this tale has some elements of Gothicism. The influence of the vampire stories of folklore and of Dr. Polidori is reflected in the eldest son's selling his blood to buy food, but in "Guzman's Family" the act by which blood becomes a means of supporting life is one of virtue rather than despicableness. The father goes mad under the force of hunger and of watching his family starve, but the madness results from undeserved suffering rather than from depraved habits. In all, Maturin's intense interest in details of inanition and suffering is of greater psychological relevance than it is of Gothic relevance.

The title character, Guzman, never appears in the story; his "family" is his sister's. She had married a Protestant music-master, Walberg, much to the fury of the Catholic Guzman. Guzman supports his sister's large family in luxury, promising to leave them his immense fortune, but he refuses to see them. When the Catholic church hides Guzman's will and claims the fortune after Guzman's death, Walberg's family is thrown into total poverty; for Walberg is unable to find work in Catholic Spain. Contrary to expectation, though, it is not Catholicism that is Maturin's subject. In fact, a "truly... good and friendly" priest, Guzman's former confessor, gives the family money from Catholic charity coffers and never slackens in his determination to prove that Guzman had not abandoned his sister's family. He succeeds, and the family returns to splendor and ease immediately after the story's climax, the excellent mad scene in which Walberg thinks he is killing his children. (They pretend to be dead.)

The bargain offered by Melmoth is of secondary importance in the narrative, though Walberg comes closer than any other of Melmoth's victims to agreeing to the terms. He thinks of doing so not because of his own sufferings but because of his children's—a kind of soul-selling that is likely to be its own absolution. Even Walberg's madness is caused not by contemplating Melmoth's offer but by the hunger of his children, which he thinks is a reproach to him.

Despite recurring sentimentality, "Guzman's Family" is grounded in reality. The forbearance of Mrs. Walberg to criticize her husband for not having better provided for possible misfortune, as well as her giving thoughtful but considerate counsel that his senile parents should not be made to go hungry, evidently attests to Maturin's strong hint in the novel's preface that she is based on his own wife. There is also, throughout the story, a healthy and unhypocritical acceptance of the importance of money. Since only Mrs. Walberg has ever seen her brother Guzman, she is the only one to grieve at his death; the others are only concerned about the money. When the will is found, restoring the Walbergs to munificence, their reaction is given without irony: "We are wealthy,—we are happy!" Likewise, the death of Walberg's mother during the period of poverty is greeted with "Thank God!" for the cessation of her suffering and for the increase in food for the survivors.

The Lovers' Tale (1660's): Even further from Gothicism than "Guzman's Family" is this tale, which deals with the great Mortimer family during the Puritan Wars, the Commonwealth, and the Restoration. Margaret, the heiress of the estate, is the Anglican daughter of a Mortimer son who had died at Newbury in the cause of Charles I. Elinor is the daughter of the second son, who had turned Puritan and married an Independent, and who had died of pleurisy through combining the professions of soldier and preacher, having given a sermon to his troops in driving rain. Their cousin John Sandal is the issue of a daughter of the Mortimer family and an Independent preacher who changed creeds as soon as he heard a new one. Of all the parents, only John's mother is still alive.

The conflict in the story develops because of the love between John and Elinor. John's mother learns that the will of the last Mortimer patriarch leaves John with only £5000 if he marries Elinor; but, if he marries Margaret, he will enjoy all of the Mortimer lands for as long as Margaret lives. On the morning of John and Elinor's wedding, Mrs. Sandal tells John that Elinor is not his cousin, but his half-sister; for her husband had committed adultery with Elinor's mother. Horrified, John rides away, not able to disgrace the memory of his father and Elinor's mother by making known what his mother has told him. Eventually, he and Margaret marry: Margaret dies in childbirth; and Mrs. Sandal repentantly tells John of her lie. Permanently deranged by the strong emotions of grief and revulsion, John spends the brief remainder of his life cared for by Elinor on her meager inheritance.

Melmoth enters, to offer his proposition to Elinor. She goes immediately to a local clergyman, who happens to have been a friend of Melmoth's in earlier days, and who had been at his bedside in Germany when he had "died." To this clergyman, Melmoth had inexplicably hinted that they might meet again; and he had enjoined him not to reveal the fact of his death (another reflection of Polidori's *The Vampyre,* whose villain had extracted the same promise from the brother of a future victim). When Melmoth is confronted by his old friend in the presence of Elinor, he walks away without a word.

Both "Guzman's Family" and "Lovers' Tale" are shot through with sentimentality. The former story has a tearful reconciliation with Walberg's parents, a daughter shrinking from prostitution as her starving parents shed tears of thanksgiving, and the extreme emotions contingent upon Walberg's insane attack on his children and his slow emergence to sanity upon being informed that the will has been found. The latter story has a superfluity of eulogy on Elinor's selfless acceptance of John's strangely treating her like a sister and her silent suffering after John's marriage to Margaret.[24] Though it lowers the quality of the narrations, sentimentality is not so disturbing here as in parts of Immalee-Isidora's tale, because in these two stories the sentimentality is not combined with implausibility but is homiletic and domestic.

Sentimentality does not seriously interfere with what Maturin does skillfully—tracing the gradual changes in character under the press of circumstances and environmental forces. The treatment of Elinor is especially noteworthy as a counterpoint to that of Eva in *Women*. As with Eva, Elinor has a conflict between religious impulse and overwhelming love for a mortal male. Love for John Sandal makes Elinor lose the "sense" of religion, though she has not lost the "hope" of it. Her sentiments imply that Maturin had intended his readers to understand that Eva died partly to preserve her sanctity from corruption by earthly love. That Elinor does not die from this conflict is evidence of *Melmoth*'s superiority to *Women* in terms of realism.[25]

Religion, which at most serves only as part of the background of oppression in "Guzman's Family," is handled in a still different basis in "The Lovers' Tale." Catholicism is never mentioned. Instead, Maturin gives a scathing picture of the absurdities of Puritanism combined with militarism, and he suggests that the psychological indecisiveness of John's preacher-father reflects the triviality of distinctions among Protestant faiths. Religious diversity is brought into proper focus by Maturin and Elinor: Maturin, as narrator, suggests that even Anglicanism can be blinding; and he adds that Elinor's is the "right conclusion": "There must be good on both sides [i.e., Puritanism and Anglicanism], however obscured or defaced by passion or interest." A reference to Mrs. Sandal's having a "false religion" is as much a criticism of her having left the religion of her birth as it is a slur on her Dissenting instability. Satire similar to that in *Women* points up the cultural poverty of Puritanism, and a portrait of an emotionless Puritan whose life is strictly regulated by the clock reinforces the idea that monastic joylessness is not solely the curse of Catholic convents. What Maturin seems most favorably disposed toward through the book as a whole is "natural" religion as contrasted to organized religion— tacitly assuming, needless to say, that Anglicanism incorporates most of the qualities of natural, unoppressed faith.

The Frame Story (concluded): Once Isidora dies at the end of "The Tale of the Indians," the novel quickly comes to its denouement.[26] Before Monçada can tell young John Melmoth the other adventures of Melmoth that he has learned from the Jew Adonijah, the Wanderer himself appears at the Irish farmhouse. He tells his horrified descendant and Monçada not to worry that he has come to destroy them. His own doom has come, his time expired. After sleeping his last human repose, Melmoth awakens tremendously aged. He warns Monçada and young John Melmoth not to come into his room no matter what noises emit. As John and Monçada listen fearfully to terrible mutterings and yells, Melmoth the Wanderer meets his fate. His body is not found; it is presumably thrown into the sea by devils from a promontory. This last part, though extremely brief, shows Maturin had not lost ability in expressing Gothic fantasies. The dream of Melmoth during his last sleep is as economical and intense as the death of the parricide or as Monçada's dream of incineration:

. . . he fell—he sunk—he blazed—he shrieked! The burning waves boomed over his sinking head, and the clock of eternity rung out its awful chime— "Room for the soul of the Wanderer!" —and the waves of the burning ocean answered, as they lashed the adamantine rock—"There is room for more!" —The Wanderer awoke.

IV   *Organizational Principles*

The great value of the last two stories—"Guzman's Family" and "Lover's Tale"— is their relationship to the earlier parts of the novel. Crucial to an understanding of the entirety of the novel and of the variety of Maturin's interests, they help us to perceive the organizational principles of the novel. The most strident horror passages come early in the book, ending, in large part, as Alonzo descends by trap door into the tunnel and finds himself in Adonijah's study-mausoleum. Maturin thereafter uses a variety of substantive material on which to base the stories which by their nature must eventuate in Melmoth's offer—Noble Savagery and initiation; the primacy of hunger and other physical needs; and finally religious-political prejudice and social arrogance.

Likewise, from the very beginning the urges of the individual characters become steadily more orthodox and "normal." Only Stanton among the victims of Melmoth is obsessed to learn Melmoth's secret; the other intended victims are sought out by the evil forces that impel Melmoth. Incorporating this progressive normalization of tone, the novel's overall movement assumes the following pattern—obsessive identification with evil (Stanton's tale); precommitted enslavement in an unnatural conventual regimen (Monçada's tale); innate bestiality of man (parricide's tale); natural goodness fascinated by but not corrupted by violent religions of blood and torture, and the ennui of barren conventional life (Immalee-Isidora's tale); religious persecution for economic reasons (Walberg's tale); and a haughty attempt to retain money in a particular branch of a family (the Mortimers' chronicle). All of these different subjects are, of course, based on the common thematic concern already discussed—the perversion of love by institutions.

Such a progression is not so facile nor so clear-cut as may appear from a simple listing. The parricide's innate bestiality finds outlets in a monastic society and is fostered by the sado-masochistic concept of Divine Judgment he has learned from observing the monks' and priests' behavior to one another; and we could argue that the parricide's form of evil is more corrosive than that of the monastery itself, at least as far as we see it during its persecution of Monçada. What Maturin does is to trace a number of common elements through the six stories: religion, monasticism, madness, responsibility, money, vanity. In each story he shifts the emphasis among these elements so that quite different configurations emerge. For example, money is nearly ignored in Stanton's story; in Monçada's story it accounts for a large measure of the ex-Jesuits' enthusiasm for Alonzo's joining their community; the parricide kills his father for money he needs to pay a gambling debt; Isidora is considered by her father and brother as a means to make a desirable mercantile alliance; Walberg's family starves for lack of money; Mrs. Sandal trades her son's happiness to gain greater wealth for him.

The one inescapable conclusion of noting the progession is that Gothicism declines while social realism increases. That much is definite, but how to account for the shifting emphases is not so easy. Perhaps Maturin's wells of Gothic inspiration were running dry; perhaps he was turning instinctively to his interest in concrete life as an integral concomitant to his interest in Gothicism. That his dependence on Gothic devices was waning may account for his forgetting to indicate in the last two stories that beautiful music accompanies Melmoth's appearance. Another explanation for the alternations in subject and tone is that Gothicism is innately limited in choice of situations. If Maturin wanted to suggest the exhaustiveness of Melmoth's search for someone to take his place or share his destiny, he could not have continued with stories like Stanton's, Alonzo's, or the parricide's without simply wearying the reader, as Lewis does in *The Monk*. By varying the subject and treatment, Maturin indirectly suggests the omnipresence of temptation to turn one's back on hope and to turn to despair. This interpretation accords with Maturin's concept of *Melmoth* as a sermon-in-fiction.

CHAPTER 6

And Yet Another Genre

THE control found in *Melmoth* is also present in *The Albigenses,*
Maturin's last novel. But in this work, his command is part of
the polish we can expect from a man who has been plying a craft
for nearly twenty years rather than, as in *Melmoth,* the result of a
cohesion of style and subject matter. This last fiction is a venture
into a genre previously unattempted by Maturin, the historical
novel. Maturin's friendship with Walter Scott has its direct literary
result in *The Albigenses.* It is not certain that he knew that Scott
was the author of the anonymously published stories by "the
author of *Waverley*"; but Scott's authorship was widely suspected
almost from the beginning of his career as a novelist. The imitation,
in any event, is not flattery or a testimony of friendship so much as
another desperate effort to benefit from a literary convention of
current popularity. Scott had dominated the historical field ever
since the publication in 1814 of *Waverley,* and the publication of
each new novel further established the salability of fiction that
used history.

Maturin's novel echoes the chivalry of Scott's *Ivanhoe, Old
Mortality,* and *Quentin Durward,* as well as the morality of
The Monastery, not to mention plot events and characters from
these and other Scott novels. Chapter mottoes are taken from
Byron's *Sardanapalus;* characters, dialogue, and scenes resemble
Shakespeare's; and allusions to the *Don Quixote* of Cervantes
abound. The extent and range of Maturin's debts to other writers
substantiate a sense of stultification of creativity in *The Albigenses*
that even the direct plagiarism of parts of Monçada's tale in *Melmoth*
does not. The plagiarized material in *Melmoth* and the novel's
Gothicism are consonant with each other and with Maturin's
genuine personal interests; the borrowings in *The Albigenses* and
its general historical bent are imposed upon each other by Maturin's
choice of what for him is an unnatural mode. A knowledge of Maturin's personal condition at the time of writing supports the internal
textual evidence that the novel was the work of a divided attention.

Maturin was still in perilous poverty, though *Melmoth* was reprinted in 1821; and by this time no hope of increased emolument from, or advancement in, the Anglican church could have remained. Most influential, however, of all the factors leading to the limitations of *The Albigenses,* was the state of Maturin's health.[1] He was failing rapidly as a result of an illness that is not specified in any record that I have seen. The seriousness of his situation is reflected in the frequent references, in the sermons being delivered during Lent of this year,[2] to the state of his health: "if health be spared"; "if life be spared"; "health long precarious, and now seriously impaired, compels me . . . to defer my task" of delivering the fifth sermon.[3] Harried also by financial problems, a sizable family, and parish duties, Maturin was forced to write *The Albigenses* in his spare time, usually by candlelight in his living room after his family had gone to bed.

Maturin intended this novel, according to the preface, to be the first book of a trilogy of "historical romances, illustrative of European feelings and manners in ancient times, in middle, and in modern." The "feudal ages" of *The Albigenses* appealed to him by " their splendid barbarism, . . . wild superstitions and dubious Christianity, their knightly gallantry and baronial oppression." An inauspicious feature of the preface is Maturin's admission that he has tried to please the critics in this novel. Cowed by previous unfavorable reception of his works, uncertain of the value of his own creative strengths, and encouraged only by his distant friend Walter Scott, it is little wonder that Maturin wrote in *The Albigenses* the least characteristic of all of his works of fiction.

I   *History and Fiction*

The historical Albigenses were a Manichean sect that had flourished near the town of Albi in southern France. As Manicheans, they held that there are two opposing creative principles in the universe, good and evil; and that all physical things are evil. Since matter is evil, Christ could not have existed in human form. Moreover, since man lives in the physical world, freeing his spirit requires conscious effort and the denial of animal appetites. Marriage, as a relationship leading to a physical union and to the creation of more physical life, was strongly disapproved of. The eating of meat was forbidden; indeed, only fruit fallen from trees was fully acceptable as food. The popularity of the sect, despite its strict asceticism, is probably due to the Albigenses' division into the "perfect" (the leaders) and the "believers" (the followers). The lives of the "believers" were much less rigidly scrutinized; and thus the religious doctrines were more easily borne.

The beliefs of the Albigenses, who were a part of a larger southern European Manichean group, the Cathari (Greek *Catharoi,* "pure"), were obviously heretical in the eyes of the Catholic church. Nonetheless the Cathari movement grew with relatively little interference from Rome during the eleventh and twelfth centuries, partly because the movement seemed part of the religious, economic, and social revival of the era. But the rapid growth of the Cathari in the last half of the twelfth century, including its establishment of a system of bishops, caused apprehension among the Catholic hierarchy, which thereupon began to institutionalize the punishment of heretics which had previously been left to the occasional impatience of vigilante Catholic citizenry. Pope Innocent III (1198–1216) pressed for legitimate conversion; but, when his legate, Peter de Castelnau, was murdered in 1208, Innocent declared a crusade against the Albigenses.

Although the Albigenses were composed largely of poor people, they were not defenseless. The most powerful noble who succoured them (more out of tolerance or indifference toward religion than out of sympathy, as well as his resentment of the challenge to his authority within his own lands posed by the Pope's forces) was Count Raymond VI of Toulouse, who indeed was suspected to have been an accessory to the assassination of Peter de Castelnau. The principal leader of the papal forces was Simon de Montfort, who cruelly crushed the Albigenses and swept through the territories of Raymond. But Montfort died in the siege of Toulouse in 1218, and Raymond's territories were restored when the Pope learned of Montfort's inhumane methods. The Albigenses were not utterly destroyed, but the growth of the group was halted. The Cathari movement, as a whole, was not completely dispelled by the Inquisition that followed the crusade; and it survived into the fifteenth century.[4]

Maturin's treatment of the history essentially accords with what is known about the Albigenses, but we could not read *The Albigen-*

ses as a substitute for a history of the period. Not only are there silent and pointless alterations, such as battle in which Simon de Montfort is killed taking place at Tarascon instead of Toulouse, and gross anachronisms, such as the reference to Montezuma (1480–1520 A.D.) in 1216; but Maturin alters the sequence of actual historical events in order to tighten the plot. For example, the wife of King Philip Augustus of France had been reconciled to her husband before 1216; but Maturin incorporates her flight from her husband into the novel to justify some of the action. Maturin usually notes his changes of history, but such admissions do not help the reader know the actual circumstances or the actual chain of events.

Maturin opens his novel in 1216, with the remark that "The crusade undertaken against the Albigenses in the reign of Philip Augustus, in the year 1208, had produced the most decisive results, and had terminated in the almost total extirpation of that people throughout the province of Languedoc." Count Raymond, who has gone to Rome to once more seek reconciliation with the Pope, has abandoned warlike preparation for the defense of a band of the remaining Albigenses, who are attempting to reach the temporarily safe kingdom of Arragon. The Albigenses' movement threatens the castle of the Lord of Courtenaye, who requests aid of Simon de Montfort. Much of the story deals with the efforts to possess the title of "champion of the church," officially held by de Montfort and sought by the Bishop of Toulouse and by Louis Dauphin of France. Of the two principal battles, both are won by the Albigeois forces. In the first, Raymond returns secretly from Rome in time to lay an ambush for the crusader knights who have arrogantly and foolishly left their men behind at the Courtenaye castle.

In this battle Simon de Montfort is seriously wounded, and a struggle for power ensues between the worldly and corrupt Bishop and the Dauphin. The struggle is climaxed but not resolved during the confrontation of the three men during an impromptu council of war in the last volume during which Simon is goaded into a furious but futile attack on the Dauphin. A tenuous reconciliation is made by the three leaders just before their combined armies hasten to battle the beleaguered Albigenses before Raymond can come again to their support. In this battle, Simon de Montfort is killed; and the crusader forces are driven to taking refuge in the castle of Tarascon. The next morning, when Raymond takes the castle, he is assisted by an exotic development in the nonhistorical plot.

II *Romance and Chivalry*

The nonhistorical plot concerns the fortunes of two noble youths, Sir Paladour de la Croix Sanglante and Amirald, and the women they love, Isabelle of Courtenaye and Genevieve, the granddaughter of the Albigeois spiritual leader Pierre, respectively. Paladour and Amirald, who are brothers, are the sons of Count Raymond who were presumed killed in infancy during a raid on their father's castle. Neither knows his ancestry; nor, having been separated during the raid, does either know that his brother is alive. Amirald, who had been "abandoned" before the gates of Courtenaye Castle, had been reared and ill-used by the Lord of Courtenaye. Wounded during the first battle and tended to health by Genevieve in a secret cave among the mountains, Amirald eventually gives allegiance to the Albigeois cause. The elder brother Paladour has sworn a sacred oath during the burning of his ancestral home to kill the last enemy of his family, though he was so young that he does not remember his family's name and thus has to trust to fate that he will be able to discover the means for revenge. Dim remembrance of the oath and the garish surroundings during his swearing it have made Paladour melancholy and resigned. (He resembles the younger Montorio brother of *Fatal Revenge;* and, of course, the idea of children unaware of their true parents also appears in Maturin's first novel.) A sorceress, who in behavior and motives resembles Schemoli of *Fatal Revenge,* appears in an ominous situation in the early part of the novel and tells Paladour that she is destined to call for the fulfillment of his oath. But she will not identify his victim until the time to perform the deed has come.

The victim turns out to be his beloved Isabelle, niece of the Lord of Courtenaye and the daughter of the previous Lord who had destroyed Paladour's home and killed his mother. The sorceress has personal reason for attempting to exact revenge on the house of Courtenaye and for using the house of Raymond as her tool. The sorceress is Marie de Mortemar, once a beautiful and wealthy girl, whose possessions had been stolen by Raymond of Toulouse, the Bishop of Toulouse, and Isabelle's father. In addition to taking her wealth because she had been suspected of being a religious heretic, the three men had misused her person in such a way that she became insane; and, casting aside pride and religious pretension, she swore she would bear any future indignities necessary to gain revenge.

Marie waits until the wedding night of Paladour and Isabelle before she demands that Paladour redeem his pledge. Rather than kill his bride or live in dishonor at breaking his vow, Paladour attempts suicide; and, in the struggle to stop him, Isabelle receives a serious wound. Paladour rushes away, thinking Isabelle is dead. Marie, with uncharacteristic ruth, decides that Count Raymond's family has suffered sufficiently by his having lost the company and affection of his sons for twenty years. She secretly nurses Isabelle back to health and installs her as a page to Paladour, in which position she can watch over Paladour and guard against the effects of his gloominess. In the novel's last battle, Marie is captured by the Bishop's forces and is scheduled to be executed with all of the prisoner Albigenses before Count Raymond can free them.

By a stratagem (Marie is unaccountably left in an unlocked room next to the chapel), Marie poisons the communion bread; and, when the Bishop says high mass before the anticipated battle, the entire garrison is destroyed. Marie gloats over the Bishop's death agonies and then pitches herself out of the castle tower to her death. Paladour and Amirald are discovered to be Raymond's sons; Paladour and Isabelle are reunited; Amirald and Genevieve receive Pierre's blessing to marry. (Throughout the novel, Maturin pays little attention to the doctrines of the Albigenses, such as their ban on marriage; but it is hardly likely that as a churchman he could have been unaware of them.)

There are many other skeins in the plot, and plot incidents, that I have left out of this sketch for clarity. Among the extended events that I have omitted are Isabelle's abduction by the outlaw Adolfo, who falls in love with her and wants to marry her instead of ransoming her; Paladour's falling into the same outlaw's power and being put into a cell with a lycanthrope (a man who thinks he's a wolf), who helps Paladour free Isabelle during one of his brief periods of lucidity but whom Paladour is forced eventually to fight in self-defense; the machinations by the Lord of Courtenaye to destroy Paladour and Amirald in fear that they will learn that it was he who had murdered their mother; and a considerable amount of complicated intrigue by Marie de Mortemar that would collapse were she not coincidentally always in the right place, as when she stabs to death the outlaw Adolpho as he is about to kill Paladour.

The effect of the interwoven activities of the fictional characters in *The Albigenses* is less obfuscating, however, than the conflux of supernaturalism and emotionalism in *Fatal Revenge*. The control given to the plot by the historical situation is beneficial, and even the implausible nonhistorical situation gains a measure of credence from the fictional characters being swept along by historical events in which they play minor directive roles.

III   *History and Chivalry*

As a historical novelist taking his lead from Walter Scott, Maturin is at best only partially successful. Unlike Scott's characters, especially those in the novels that portray the nearly contemporary history of the eighteenth century, Maturin's central nonhistorical characters express only vaguely the attitudes of the times or of the groups of which they form a part. Even Genevieve, as a member of the persecuted minority, says nothing to the point; indeed, she would seem to be no more heretical than the meekest parishioner in Maturin's own church. Moreover, with the exception of the contrast between the saintly pastor Pierre and the fanatical Albigeois leaders such as Mattathias, the warrior, and Boanerges, the preacher, there is little doctrinal distinction among the Albigenses; even the Catholics distinguish the Albigenses' despicableness only by noting that they are "heretics."[5]

In Scott, there is a layer of serious intellectual interchange, for the Scot rebel is wont to argue his position against a Scot or an Englishman reconciled to the Hanoverian claim; but Maturin's created characters reveal themselves to be without settled social and religious convictions when they are caught in a personal dilemma. Both Paladour and Amirald move from the Pope's forces to those of the Albigenses. Amirald's shift is carried out with some attention to motivation: he is torn between the simplicity of Genevieve's life and the grand world of chivalry. Likewise, Paladour's shift is not without psychological cause; but he seems basically unaware of the significance of his religious allegiance, though such matters were of course important in the world of chivalry. Wishing only to find death because he thinks he has killed his wife, but beseeched by the sorceress not to raise his lance against Raymond, he joins Raymond's army. But even Amirald's change is not made smoothly: in one chapter he swears total fealty to his liege the Dauphin even though the Dauphin will not renounce his intention to make the captive Genevieve his mistress. Amirald in effect thereby countenances the dishonor of his beloved and thus makes clear his sense of the comparative force of feudal and romantic obligations. But in the next chapter Amirald—who in the meantime has rescued Genevieve from a Catholic mob—joins the Albigeois forces and tells them of the crusaders' strategy of attack and thus breaks the solemn vows of feudal allegiance to the Dauphin which he had just renewed.

Maturin seems to have diagnosed Scott's popularity as based on the portrayal of chivalrous action, whether the scene be the Middle Ages or the Border Country of the eighteenth century. There are certainly generic similarities between Ivanhoe and the brothers Paladour and Amirald, despite the intensified artificiality of Paladour and Amirald. All three abide by an elaborate code of manners that could not be perfectly followed by a mortal being. But Maturin's talents fail him in making a context for his heroes; the details of Ivanhoe's bearing and actions, and his sense of identity with a moral code as well as with a courtly etiquette, create a degree of verisimilitude that Amirald and Paladour fall short of.

The effect of Maturin's portrayal of chivalry is doubly unfortunate because it coincides with his natural propensity, previously seen especially in *The Milesian Chief*, to create superheroes, whose reality is inevitably falsified by their flowery diction and pompous sentiments. *The Milesian Chief* survives, if in a limited sense, because the female foil has a complex life that modifies the moral perfection and ideal qualities of Connal O'Morven. But in *The Albigenses*, Genevieve and especially Isabelle contribute to the artificiality of characterization. Paladour in particular, but Amirald nearly as starchly, makes his way through life abiding by innumerable conventions of the most flaccid sentimental-historical fiction. He accepts a challenge to be Isabelle's champion in a joust with the powerful Simon de Montfort "with blushing and deferential awe to the fair being for whom he was perilling fame and life." When asked by Isabelle, "Who watches [is awake] at this late hour?," Paladour answers, "It is your beauty's servant and everwakeful meditator." When de Montfort blames himself because the crusader knights without their supporting men face certain death in the Albigenses' ambush, Paladour puts aside his enmity to express his feudal loyalty: " 'Now foul befall the tongue that reproaches thee in an hour like this, noble de Montfort!' said the generous Paladour; 'for surely it was the noble heat of a true valour that lighted the flame that must consume us this day.' "

Isabelle, like Paladour, is beyond the reader's imaginative iden-tification. Unlike Genevieve, who, because she is a fugitive heretic, is threatened with rape by one character after another, Isabelle experiences only one encounter with the coarseness of feudal life, and that vaguely, with the outlaw chief. He is suitably chastened by her reaction: "His inflamed eyes menaced more than scorn, and he seemed advancing to fulfil their threat. . . . At this moment, a slight but determined movement of the lady Isabelle (who half-started from her seat), her compressed lips, and the fixed and fearful bending of her eye on the walls of her prison [evidently portending suicide], made the bold outlaw shrink before her." When Adolpho proposes marriage to Isabelle in defiance of the difference in their social rank, he is again cowed by her sense of the outrage he is com-mitting by merely thinking that they could make an equal union: "Isabelle sprang on her feet— both hands were compressed on her left bosom, as if *expecting* her heart would burst, and her eyes inflamed and dilated seemed starting from their sockets. . . . The outlaw, with all his atrocious boldness, was daunted at the sight: he rushed from her apartment, cursing the very pride to which he crouched."

The historical characters fare much better. Probably because only ruthless men with a strong streak of ego could stand above the prejudices of the era and remain visible through the dimming effect of seven centuries, and because evil is more engrossing in narrative than virtue, the Bishop of Toulouse affords an opportunity for powerful characterization that calls forth Maturin's finest powers. His personality dominates any event in which he takes part, especially during the confrontation between him and the Dauphin, and then during the confrontation of the ill Simon de Montfort facing the Bishop and the Dauphin, who have intuitively put aside their mutual loathing in order to meet Simon's challenge. Even though Maturin's portrayal of the Bishop as incredibly successful in battle (he kills an enemy with each swing of his sword during the ambush) is as false as the similar portrayal of Paladour and Amirald, the analysis of him as a clear-sighted man who works upon the susceptible, illiterate knights and feudal leaders in order to fulfill his own ambitions is well done. In a similar manner, Simon is a sound portrait of a physically powerful, mentally limited man who has gained eminence by his martial ability and by his cruelty but who can be goaded by a clever man such as the Bishop into an attack upon his future sovereign. The Dauphin is a libertine of the same cut as the Pretender in Thackeray's *Henry Esmond,* although, as is perhaps fitting for a rougher age, the Dauphin is willing to rape if efforts at seduction fail.

One of the more attractive features of *The Albigenses* is the honesty with which it handles social conditions during the era it presents. In few instances does Maturin palliate the crudity and violence of life during the thirteenth century. He is only slightly reticent about the rape and infamous treatment of Marie de Mortemar, the threats to Genevieve, and the licentious and drunken conduct of the knights. The great amount of interest shown in chastity and in lewd living is no doubt partly an effort by Maturin to appeal to his readers as much as a desire to be historically truthful. But such honesty still compensates for the preponderance of chivalric artificiality of manners when Isabelle and Paladour are present.

IV   *The Gothic Element*

Despite Maturin's desperate and conscientious efforts to write a historical and chivalric novel, he could not entirely put aside his *métier,* the fantastic. Nor could he avoid the expansive and intro-spective painting of the concrete that creates an aura of the super-natural and mysterious. But battle and history do not lend themselves readily to Maturin's brand of Gothic treatment. *The Albigenses* is not a historical Gothic novel, in the manner of either Clara Reeve's *Old English Baron* or Thomas Leland's *Longsword, Earl of Salis-bury* (1762), but a novel in which history and Gothicism conflict with each other. The effectiveness of the one genre (a quasi-factual account of man's condition at a given point in time) works against that of the other (an imaginative heightening of fears of the unknown in life).

Marie de Mortemar poses as a sorceress; the Lord of Courtenaye keeps a retinue of witches; there is a night of ghost tales at Courtenaye Castle; and an aghast Genevieve sees the supposedly dead Isabelle standing near her bier (Isabelle's "burial" being part of Marie de Mortemar's plan to install her as Paladour's page). The sense of horror is partially dispelled by attempts at humor; a sequence during which Paladour is supposedly being put through a fearful test by Marie and the witches is presented only indirectly, through two foppish and superstitious knights who hide under the coverlets of their beds when they hear a scream that pierces the floors of the castle. As is usual with Maturin, the most effective Gothic bits are evocations of states of mind beyond the comfort of conscience. The Lord of Courtenaye, who wishes to serve the devil, uses language that on one occasion approaches that of *Fatal Revenge* in trying to convince Marie de Mortemar to introduce him to Satan: "I tell thee, it [the sight of Satan] is the unquenchable thirst of my spirit. The spirit that works within me needs a mightier one to strive with for mastery or subjection. Let me behold, if thou hast such power, my vassal or my chief. I would behold at once the entrance to that lower world and its dark and potent ruler, such as thou hast painted him!" In a similar vein, the description of Genevieve's reaction to the sight of the "dead" Isabelle in her shroud: "The hair of her flesh stood up—every pore tingled with distinct vitality—her eyes became, to her own perception, glazed, though she retained the full power of vision; the next moment they were dilated beyond her power of closing them; the figure appeared expanding in dimensions and advancing on her. . . . The air became tremulous with a purple light."

A small amount of the Gothicism in the novel shows Maturin simply whetting the reader's curiosity. One instance of this sort of thing is the blood on Paladour's armor the morning after his first, nocturnal encounter with Marie. She has posed as a mysterious "lady of the lake" who ferries him alone across a lake one gloomy night. During the trip, she tells him that she knows of his oath and has come to claim its fulfillment. The cause of the blood is never explained.

The absence of genuine or sustained supernaturalism does not prevent Maturin from decorating the novel with effective Gothic trappings. The description of the outlaw Adolpho's castle on an island is in the best Radcliffean manner, with secret passageways and with thundering waves crashing on the island's base far below the ramparts. Most striking, though, is the lycanthrope, one of the most garish products of Maturin's flamboyant imagination, and one of the earliest appearances in English fiction of the werewolf. The lycanthrope is strikingly presented, bearing in his hand food snatched from "the grave" and attacking Paladour in his sleep. Still, the frightening deportment of the man-wolf is quite different from the horrors in *Fatal Revenge,* whose mysteries are not explained until the novel's end. Maturin seems almost eager to rationalize and intellectualize the existence of the "fiend" in Adolpho's dungeon rather than attempt to sustain interest in the inexplicability of evil.

V   *The Religion of Tolerance*

The Albigenses, not free of slanted scenes, contains some sharp if humorous criticisms of the medieval sale of indulgences; but in its entirety it presents a balanced view of religious faiths. Compared to *Melmoth, The Albigenses* is tolerant of Catholicism. But, of course, it needs to be remembered that Maturin, as an Anglican, could have claimed as part of his own religious tradition the Catholic church of the thirteenth century. He could well have seen the beliefs of the Albigenses as contrary to his own articles of faith, even though, as I have observed, he does not stress the doctrines of the Albigenses; he only vaguely refers to the Albigenses as precursors of English Puritans "centuries later."

Maturin generally favors neither Catholicism nor Albigenseanism; rather, he isolates individual adherents of either creed for praise or criticism. Pierre, the blind leader of the Albigenses, is kind and gentle-mannered; indeed, his influence on the Albigenses has been intentionally curtailed by the militaristic Mattathias and Boanerges. On the Catholic side, the Monk of Montcalm, the mediator sent by the Pope to try to curb the Bishop's intolerance and ambition, is concerned for the spiritual health of the Albigenses and tries to convert them by reason and prayer.

Maturin's criticism is leveled primarily at the fanatics of both sides of the dispute, such as Boanerges; the opportunists, such as the

Bishop of Toulouse and Mephibosheth; and the psychological aberrants, such as the Abbot of Normoutier and Mattathias. Maturin opposes the cruel excesses and persecution and torture practiced by both of the groups. He satirizes both Catholicism's amorality, typified by the Bishop and the Abbot, and Albigensianism's hypocrisy and weakness of flesh, as seen most clearly in Mephibosheth's joining the monks at Normoutier in a riotous "revel of misrule" and in his ultimately becoming converted to monastic Catholicism after eating sumptuous food from the Bishop's kitchen. Though Count Raymond is by no means a spokesman for Maturin, his vacillations indicate at least part of Maturin's view of the disputants: "—now indignantly opposing the superstitions and the domination of the Church of Rome,—now revolted by the enthusiasm and daring pretensions of the Albigeois: —such was Raymond of Toulouse."

It is pertinent that Maturin portrays the monks in the Abbot of Normoutier's establishment as little different from the Albigenses and no different from the laymen who are only nominal Catholics. The "revel of misrule" enjoyed during the abbot's absence primarily involves only gluttony, drinking, and high-jinks (until Mephibosheth destroys carvings of saints); in other words, the oppressed monks imitate their unworthy leader's way of life. Monks kidnap Genevieve as an offering for the Abbot of Normoutier, but so do knights, for the Dauphin; in a similar manner, outlaws kidnap Isabelle for their chieftain Adolpho. Maturin points out that the Cathari heresy gave cause for the establishment of the Inquisition, but *The Albigenses* contains no Catholic characters who would enjoy the role of an Inquisitor; and in this respect they are unlike the various clerics in *Melmoth* who would find in such a role the pleasure and the capstone of their careers.

Maturin's presentation, however, tends to favor the Albigenses, probably because the Albigenses are humble people while the Catholic crusaders are frequenters of courts and given to intrigue from habit as much as from a necessity for staying alive. Maturin pointedly draws a contrast between the mourning of an Albigensian mother for her son and that of the Countess de Montfort for her husband. Morally, the Albigensian's grief is higher; for she is concerned with her son's soul; but the Countess swears that the blood of "a thousand churls" will fall for every drop of her hus-

band's, "and Christendom shall see [my] oath fulfilled." (Part of
the effectiveness of this contrast, of course, relies on the sentimental
concept of the moral superiority of the poor.) Moreover, while
Maturin can praise the "fearless humanity" of Catholic monks
who save Genevieve's life during a blizzard in the mountains,
a rhetorically more powerful depiction of his concept of Catholicism
is the Bishop of Toulouse's speech to Genevieve as he attempts to
persuade her to become his mistress. The Bishop boasts that the
Church of Rome enslaves men's minds—not merely bodies as did
the old Roman Empire. He says that the Church sanctifies murder and
rebellion and that it is beyond morality since it has the power to
declare what is good and what is evil. That such views grossly distort
all religions—not just that of the speaker—suggests a degree of
blind loathing of Roman Catholicism on Maturin's part for which
the Bishop's opportunism is not responsible. But this sort of scorn
toward Catholicism is infrequent in *The Albigenses*.

CHAPTER 7

Success and Failure

TO place Maturin finally in his appropriate niche in the literary history of England or of Western Europe is not yet possible. Though he has been dead for nearly a century and a half, an assessment of his importance cannot be made until the movements in which he took part have received more intensive study. The always increasing interest in W. B. Yeats and Oscar Wilde seems not to have led to any thorough examination of their far-distant Irish predecessors; and the contemporary context in which Maturin wrote *The Wild Irish Boy, The Milesian Chief,* and *Women* remains largely unknown.

The prospects that his contribution to Gothic literature will be weighed in the near future are greater. Gothic literature appears to be in for a revival, not only with writers of fiction themselves who for years have used Gothicism within a larger scope, such as Faulkner, Flannery O'Connor, Shirley Jackson, and Evelyn Waugh, but more recently within the graduate schools, which are the places where the research necessary for us to eventually understand Maturin's place is the most likely to be done. It may be that this academic interest in Gothicism is purely pragmatic, as doctoral candidates lunge desperately, as a last resort for a topic, into a period that has not been exhaustively discussed.

It is more likely, though, that the renewed interest in Gothicism, both artistic and scholarly, is the result of the condition that our country is rapidly becoming aware that it is in. The computer may be replacing the church and repressive government as the symbol of a regimented life; air and water pollution may be presenting as serious a problem to our accustomed ways of life as did the Industrial Revolution in Maturin's time; the discoveries about ourselves taught us by Sigmund Freud and Alfred Kinsey may be having as profound an effect on our writers' perspectives and choices of topics as did the revelations of Rousseau and the Marquis de Sade. However that may be, it is clear that the literary world has moved far beyond the sanity and balance of the Victorians who

succeeded Maturin and the other early nineteenth-century Gothicists, and that it has carried the experiments into the techniques of
fiction, ones that have concerned writers from James Joyce to
Robbe-Grillet, about as far as the experiments can be taken.

Writers are, therefore, moving back to basic human issues, to
frontal confrontations with psychological concerns—confrontations
that place such diverse modern writers as Philip Roth, Kurt
Vonnegut, and Joyce Carol Oates into the same posture toward
experience that Maturin and Lewis had. It is not customary to
think of Gothic writers as great realists because their portrayals
of character so frequently are rank with sentimentalism and their
portrayals of action filled with implausibilities. Yet they were
realistic in their perception of the depths in the human personality,
as I have tried to indicate in several places in dealing with Maturin.
Modern writers are also probing into the depths; the agonized
self-loathing and self-infatuation of Roth's Portnoy are not very
far from Melmoth's determination to curse another soul because
of the greatness of his own self-loathing, nor from the other Gothic
hero-villains' mixed self-lacerations and self-aggrandizements.

When the final assessment of Gothic masters can be made, Maturin
will certainly be awarded a high place. It is unlikely that his work
will be denigrated, whatever standards are applied, whatever more
is learned about the period and about the other writers. If Maturin
had written nothing but *Melmoth,* he would have been a formidable
figure in English Gothicism. But he also wrote other novels in which
Gothicism plays an important function, and he helped to develop
a uniquely English hero-villain in Gothic drama. Indeed, his work
might well be seen, when the definitive evaluation of Gothicism is
made, as the paradigm of the Gothic effort.

For neither Maturin's life, nor English Gothicism, was everything it might have been. Unlike modern Gothic writers, who have
the philosophical system of Existentialism and the esthetic tradition
of Surrealism to dignify their distortions of "real" life, Maturin
and his fellow early Gothicists carried out their intuitions about
the nature of personality and about the quality of life under a repressive social system without a narrative tradition that they
could feel was adequate for everything they wanted it to do. They
simply trusted to making it do as much as they could, not worrying
overmuch (if at all) about contradictions in time or about im-

plausibilities of action and character. The conventions of sentimentalism they accepted, unquestioningly in most cases, in much the same way that modern Gothic writers—and most other modern writers as well—accept those of ironic understatement and philosophic skepticism.

Another quality in Maturin's career makes him a peculiarly poignant example of the artist caught between modes of literary expression and between the demands of art and practical life: his career is a painful illustration of the dilemma that a man of genius confronts when his genius neither fully accords with existing fashions nor is unique enough to require him to develop new forms in which to express himself. His dramas and his novels evince Maturin's individualistic handling of his materials; but there is also an acquiescence in his audience's expectations from the form he was imitating. In a few works, especially in *Bertram* and *Melmoth,* the forms were congenial to his personal manner of expression and experimentation; and he produced masterpieces of the forms. In other cases, as with *Fatal Revenge, The Milesian Chief,* and *Women,* the forms require exertions of secondary or transient impulses—Radcliffean supernaturalism, sensationalization of recent Irish history, and social wit. He produced adequate examples of the forms, but only *Fatal Revenge* rises above mediocrity. In still other cases, as with *The Wild Irish Boy* and *The Albigenses,* he was not only imitating genres but manufacturing an interest on his own part in his material; and, while the works may fulfill some of the requirements of the form and may contain characteristics of Maturin, they are largely devoid of literary value.

Maturin's work is uneven; the promise of an original prose style in *Fatal Revenge* materialized only fitfully until *Melmoth the Wanderer. Melmoth* is a masterpiece of Gothic writing—of its quality there is no question. A permanent triumph exists also in Maturin's life and work: he determinedly experimented in a genre that seemed falling out of popular favor because of his inner recognition that the Gothic was the mode closest to his own capabilities. To provide the culmination of a widespread literary activity is not a contemptible achievement.

Notes and References

Chapter One

1. So unanimously report his contemporary biographers, but an examination of the records of St. Peter's parish results in a less certain evaluation. His name as presiding clergyman first appears in the vestry books for April 15, 1805, in a wedding entry, and thereafter irregularly and sporadically. He first officiated at a vestry meeting, one of the duller of clerical obligations, on June 10, 1809—more than four years after he had begun at St. Peter's. Once he settled into his work, he performed a good proportion of the clerical duties at St. Peter's, although never as much as the other curates, John Lewis and John Webb. It should be noted that the records of St. Peter's only indicate who performed ceremonies and signed documents, and do not necessarily reflect the proportion of other parish duties that Maturin carried out. His statement to Scott in 1813 that his duties were principally confined to Sunday must be read in the context of the letter, in which he assures Scott that he has time for other work; *The Correspondence of Sir Walter Scott and Charles Robert Maturin: With a Few Other Allied Letters,* eds. Fannie E. Ratchford and Wm. H. McCarthy Jr. (Austin, Texas, 1937), p. 14; henceforth cited as *Scott-Maturin Correspondence.*

2. Maturin's income from tutoring varied enormously; one year he made £1000, the next year only £500, the next year nothing (*ibid.,* pp. 20, 34). His curate's living was worth about £75 a year, and until 1817 he and his fellow curates were each paid an extra £50 a year for performing the Sunday services.

3. [Sir Walter Scott], *"Fatal Revenge; or, the Family of Montorio,"* Quarterly Review, III (May, 1810), 339–47.

4. Manuscript in the possession of John Murray, Ltd., of London; dated August 19, 1816.

5. The nature and extent of this debt is the major biographical issue in Maturin's life, for he used it frequently as an excuse for his poverty and for his writing hastily. On May 11, 1819, in a letter to his publisher Constable, Maturin, pleading for an advance on *Melmoth* of £250, refers to "the cruel and oppressive extravagance of my own brother," and says "the present claim is *the last* that can ever be urged against me on that unworthy account"; Constable Letter Books, National Library of Scotland MS 673, ff. 35–36.

Few bankruptcy records of this period survived the fire that gutted the

Public Records Office building (Four Courts) in Dublin in 1922 during the Insurrection. The only surviving record of a lawsuit involving a Maturin lists Arnold and Elizabeth Eggers as plaintiffs against Gabriel Maturine. The case's resolution is not given in the Bill Book, which means, according to the Keeper of the Public Records, that the case was probably settled out of court. There is no direct evidence that this case concerns the debt for which Maturin became responsible; and family genealogical records do not clearly indicate Gabriel's relationship to Charles Robert's family. The bill was entered in the Bill Book on December 2, 1809, a month after Maturin's father lost his position as Clerk of the Munster Road; it is not unlikely that Gabriel Maturin's creditors descended as soon as his relative's ability to stand by him ended.

6. See n. 5, ch. 4.

7. Maturin's use of Irish nationalism and Wordsworthian Romanticism is discussed by H. W. Piper and A. Norman Jeffares in "Maturin the Innovator," *Huntington Library Quarterly,* XII (1958), 261–84. An extremely interesting contemporary summary of Maturin's career uses Coleridge's distinctions of Imagination, Reason, and Fancy in order to isolate Maturin's qualities; [T. Noon Talfourd], "On the Living Novelists: Maturin," *New Monthly Magazine,* XIV (August, 1820), 142–47, esp. 144–45.

8. Maturin's basic position as expressed in *Five Sermons of the Errors of the Roman Catholic Church* (1824) is that evidence in the Bible undercuts the authority of tradition and the temporal Body claimed by the Roman Catholic church. Sermons II and III deny the validity of all the sacraments except Baptism and Marriage; Sermon IV uses sophistry to argue that the Roman Catholic church is not apostolic; and Sermon V recapitulates the earlier sermons. Maturin is not systematic as an analyst and interpreter of doctrine. He proceeds instinctively, following Anglican orthodoxies but becoming hopelessly snarled whenever he tries to resolve subtle distinctions.

9. See Sister Mary Muriel Tarr, *Catholicism in Gothic Fiction: A Study of the Nature and Function of Catholic Materials in Gothic Fiction in England (1762-1820)* (Washington, D.C., 1956).

10. The legendary activities of the Inquisition gave birth to the motif of the secret society, a major contribution by the German Gothic writers.

11. Montague Summers, *The Gothic Quest* (London, 1938), pp. 398–400, carefully argues the former view; Devendra P. Varma, *The Gothic Flame* (London, 1957), pp. 216–19, the latter.

12. Varma (pp. 135–39) places Godwin among the *Schauer-Romantik.* But Godwin's bias in rationality merits a separate classification.

13. Robert D. Mayo, "How Long was Gothic Fiction in Vogue?," *Modern Language Notes,* LVIII (January, 1943), 58–64.

Chapter Two

1. Penciled note on Maturin's letter to Longman's inquiring into the number of unsold stock; this information was furnished me by Dr. James C. Corson, owner of the letter.

2. Niilo Idman, *Charles Robert Maturin: His Life and Works* (London, 1923), p. 15.

3. Edith Birkhead, *The Tale of Terror: A Study of the Gothic Romance* (London, 1921), p. 82.

4. Ernest Baker, *The History of the English Novel* (London, 1929), V, 220.

5. Scott, *Quarterly Review*, 343; and Idman, p. 43.

6. According to James B. Leslie, *Dublin Clergy Succession*, II (unpublished; only known copy is in the Library of the Representative Body of the Church of Ireland, Dublin), Maturin kept a school from 1807 to 1813. But this entry on Maturin is wrong on a number of points—e.g., in saying Maturin did not begin his curacy at St. Peter's until 1817—so its dating of Maturin's tutoring cannot be accepted confidently.

7. *The Satirist*, II (1807), 531.

8. Idman, p. 64.

9. Thomas Flanagan, *The Irish Novelists, 1800–1850* (New York, 1959), pp. 119, 121–23. Another study of Owenson is Lionel Stevenson, *The Wild Irish Girl: The Life of Sydney Owenson, Lady Morgan (1776–1859)* (London, 1936).

10. Flanagan, p. 111.

11. Oliver Elton's description of Connal as a mythic hero well communicates the reason he is the least satisfactory element in a novel with a basis in a realistic situation. He "is not only a martyr-rebel, but an unreal Ossianic hero, descended from the 'ancient bards'; not an Irishman of any known variety"; *Survey of English Literature* (New York, 1912), I, 218.

12. Idman (p. 92) thinks Wandesford as a man of the world is the best-drawn male character in the book. It seems to me that Idman overlooks the stereotypical aspects of Wandesford—the army officer cowardly in private danger, the insatiable vindictive hatred of the morally superior Connal. Idman fails to note the originality of Desmond's strong expressions of physical emotion and the complexities of his motivation.

Chapter Three

1. Harold Child, *The Cambridge History of English Literature*, eds. A. W. Ward and A. R. Waller (London, 1917), XIII, 283–85.

2. See Allardyce Nicoll, *A History of English Drama 1660–1900* (New York, 1948), IV, 51–55, for details on author's remuneration.

3. Bertrand Evans denies that the heroic drama was a precursor to the Gothic drama in *Gothic Drama from Walpole to Shelley* (Berkeley and Los Angeles, 1947), p. 18. But that heroic and Gothic drama are distinct forms does not preclude relationships, influences, and borrowings. Evans himself traces a resemblance from the heroic Almanzor to John Home's *Douglas* (1757) and from there to the hero of Gothic dramas (p. 25); and he explicitly names heroic drama as one of several sources of ideas for Gothic dramatists (p. 190). One of Maturin's biographers asserts that Lee's *Alexander* was Maturin's favorite play; "Conversations of Maturin. —No. II," *New Monthly Magazine*, XIX (June, 1827), 574.

4. Nearly all of the reviewers discuss *Bertram* as a tragedy: *Monthly Review*, CLXI (June, 1816), 185; *British Review*, VIII (August, 1816), 80–81; *Eclectic Review*, MDCCCXVI (October, 1816), 379; and esp. *British Critic*, V (May, 1816), 502. Even Samuel Taylor Coleridge, who is very sarcastic about the play, discusses it in relation to accepted tragedies; *Biographia Literaria*, ed. J. Shawcross (Oxford, 1907), II, 181–93. The twentieth century also recognizes the seriousness of Maturin's goals. Allardyce Nicoll discusses Maturin's works under the category of "Tragedies and Dramas" in *A History of English Drama*, IV, 166–67, 176.

5. William Hazlitt, reviewing for *The Examiner*, IX (May 19, 1816), 313, calls *Bertram* a "modern romantic tragedy," denying it is a tragedy "in the best sense of the word." "Romantic" and "Gothic" are often used as synonyms in contemporary reviews. Hazlitt clearly means "Gothic": he says that this kind of tragedy "courts distress, affects horror, indulges in all the luxury of woe."

6. I have not attempted to sort out the influences of the "German school" of sentiment and horror and the French *mélodrame* upon the English Gothic drama or upon Maturin. These Continental dramas are customarily considered to be extremely forceful influences; but Bertrand Evans puts a strong case for circular influence. He summarizes:

We have seen [pp. 116–30 of his book] how English materials developed in Germany under various forces peculiar to that country and returned, with interest accrued, to England. Similarly, in France, works of the Gothicists were quickly received, developed under such forces as Rousseauism and the Revolution, and came back to England in adaptations of Pixérécourt and others. By the end of the first decade of the new century, French, German, and English materials had become international baggage, and some works were battered from much travel. (Evans, p. 164)

Maturin himself abjures "the heresies of a false taste founded on the French drama"; *Scott-Maturin Correspondence*, p. 80. Claiming it was "vain to write good poetry for the stage," he intentionally wrote bombast in *Manuel*, which he termed "the greatest melodrame that ever was acted, whatever be its other *demerits*" (*ibid.*, p. 70).

The distinctive qualities of French *mélodrame* are the *scène lyrique* and the pantomime accompanied by music; Evans, pp. 162–63. To these were added merely the standard Gothic machinery. The contributions of the Germans were secret tribunals, an intense interest in black magic, evil monks, and variations of dangers such as trapdoors and travelers meeting disaster by taking refuge in a castle during a storm. German drama had a strong impact on the English Gothic novel—especially Lewis' and Maturin's—but not on English Gothic drama (*ibid.*, pp. 116–30). The only effect of the sentimental plays of Kotzebue, according to Evans, is that, because they came from Germany at the same time that the German Gothic plays did, they helped to obscure the genuine nature of the English Gothic drama (pp. 130–31).

7. Maturin told Scott that he feared damage to his clerical and pedagogical professions if his authorship of a play became known, so he did not submit the manuscript to the Dublin dramatic manager; *Scott-Maturin Correspondence*, p. 37. His fears were later substantiated by recurring rumors and newspaper reports that he was in danger of being suspended from his Church living for having written *Bertram* (*ibid.*, pp. 58, 61, 64). A reviewer of *Melmoth* reports that the suspension had actually occurred; *Monthly Review*, CLXXV (January, 1821), 83; but his report was inaccurate. Maturin was not suspended, and as far as the surviving diocese records reveal, he was never officially reprimanded.

Indeed, in 1819 the Archdeacon of Dublin (who was also the incumbent Vicar of St. Peter's) offered to let Maturin use the "castle-frank" to send the manuscript of *Sermons* to Constable in Edinburgh. Since postage was very expensive at this time, the Archdeacon's offer is noteworthy. In a letter to Constable (January 25, 1819), Maturin noted that the frank applies only to "MS of *that description*" (i.e., theological, not imaginative, writing). It is true that after 1816 Maturin no longer received the extra £50 from St. Peter's "for performing divine services"; but since the other curates also lost this supplement to their stipend it is not certain whether its discontinuance reflects disapproval of Maturin's literary work.

8. According to *Scott-Maturin Correspondence*, p. 65, this period was occupied by Maturin in numerous literary activities, including an unfinished comedy. Letters to John Murray indicate he also wrote *Manuel* during this time; Murray letters, dated August 19 and November 19, 1816.

9. Box of newspaper clippings concerning the Drury Lane Theater in 1816; British Museum shelfmark C.120.h.l. Clipping dated May 19, 1816. A near-identical clipping, hand-dated May 26, reports the royal visit and adds, "The new tragedy acts better than at first."

10. *Biographia Literaria*, II, 206. Coleridge's savage attack, to which the infuriated Maturin intended a riposte until Walter Scott convinced him that to reply would only alert more people to the existence of Coleridge's essay, is generally attributed to Coleridge's anger that his play *Zapolya*

had been rejected by Drury Lane in favor of *Bertram*. A second cause of his ire could well have been a combined review of *Bertram* and *Christabel* in *The British Review*, VIII (August, 1816), 64–81. The judgment was that *Christabel* is "a weak and singularly nonsensical and affected performance; but the play of *Bertram* is a production of undoubted genius."

11. Coleridge, II, 202; *Monthly Review*, 179–80; *British Review*, 79; *British Critic*, 508; *Eclectic Review*, 379; *Dublin Examiner*, 1 (September, 1816), 385–86.

12. Coleridge (II, 192–93) calls it a "Jacobinical drama," that tries to "*reconcile* us to vice and want of principle." A later critic says the play's "immoral tendency" shortened the duration of its stage run; "Recollections of Maturin–No. IV," *New Monthly Magazine*, XX (October, 1827), 375. A reviewer of *Melmoth* says that the immoral tone of *Bertram* is the "most serious charge against Mr. Maturin" five years after the play's first production; "On the Writings of Mr. Maturin, and More Particularly his 'Melmoth'," *The London Magazine*, III (May, 1821), 516. See also *Scott-Maturin Correspondence*, p. 90.

13. A reviewer of *Manuel* remarks that *Bertram* did not merely expose guilt, but also decorated it; *Monthly Review*, CLXIV (August, 1817), 392. The same reviewer thinks that "other modern plays" share this tendency.

14. There is also a very practical justification for this speech. Had Bertram not expressed contrition for his adultery, the Lord Chamberlain probably would not have licensed the production.

15. The ending of the original manuscript (see pp. 70–71) shows Bertram planning to die fighting. His death, at the hands of the Dark Knight the Forest, occurs off-stage.

16. The reviewer for the *British Critic*, 507–8, is outraged at the idea that the audience is supposed to admire Bertram's "magnificence of mind" to the very end, including the suicide. He includes Byron's heroes in his attack on antisocial heroes. (In fiction, Schedoni in *The Italian* also dies an unrepentant suicide. Unlike the hero-villain Bertram, however, Schedoni is always the villain, and so there is no ambiguity of morality.)

17. The Prior's aside—"For sterner oft our words than feelings are"— partially palliates this excoriation; and in the original manuscript, a final scene with Imogine displays him more sympathetically. But, in all, his eccentric behavior dominates.

18. E.g., Idman, p. 119.

19. Evans, pp. 86–89, 182.

20. See also Byron's *Cain* (1821), III, 11. 509–10.

21. A contemporary Irish writer generally enthusiastic at his countryman's success in London was nonplussed at Maturin's faulty morality. He acceded that Imogine's infidelity is partially excusable in that she had been forced to marry Aldobrand; but Bertram does not suffer for his

crimes, and indeed "the crimes themselves are the consummation of his happiness"; *Dublin Examiner,* 387.

22. One needs to note the similarity between the regret for seducing Imogine that Bertram expresses immediately after the seduction, and the agony he feels at seeing the insane Imogine at the play's end. The former emotion has no reference to immorality, only to Imogine's "innocence," and the latter is entirely personal.

23. In nondramatic Gothic-Romantic literature one can point to Byron's Childe Harold as a predecessor to Bertram who feels no guilt. But, of course, Harold's sins are almost entirely mere sexual peccadilloes.

24. Evans, pp. 196–97.

25. *Ibid.,* p. 237, points to an innocent man who thinks he is guilty—the hero of Lewis' *Adelmorn, the Outlaw* (1801)—as one variation of the tradition. Bertram's unwarranted assumption of his own innocence is another variation.

26. Kean, in fact, thought that Imogine's was the most effective part. But Imogine was not played by an experienced actress like Mrs. Siddons who might eclipse him, so Kean took the role and studied to make Bertram "the most conspicuous object in the play;" "Rev. Charles Robert Maturin," *Irish Quarterly Review,* V (March, 1852), 151–52. Kean's feelings on this point may account for *Bertram* being played only four times in 1817; but it might not have been played at all except that Kean was forced to find a tragedy to replace *Manuel,* which failed.

27. Surviving letters from Lamb to Maturin indicate that the new portions written by Lamb are all minor, that the majority of new sections were written by Maturin; *Scott-Maturin Correspondence,* pp. 41–47, 56. After the play was produced, Maturin complained bitterly to Scott that *Bertram* had been *"un-Maturined,"* but he seems to be referring only to the excision of the dark knight (*ibid.,* p. 59), to which he had tacitly agreed.

28. *Edinburgh Review,* XXX (June, 1818), 254–56. See also his letter to Maturin, *Scott-Maturin Correspondence,* pp. 30–31.

29. See n. 27 above.

30. *The Examiner,* X (March 16, 1817), 175. Idman (p. 137) says that the madness of Manuel in the last act is "insupportable" and that Kean could hardly be blamed.

31. A letter dated November 21 [1817], evidently to Archibald Constable, complains he has not been paid what is owing him from *Manuel;* Constable Letter Books, National Library of Scotland MS 2224, f. 79. Maturin understood the terms of a playwright's compensation (see *Scott-Maturin Correspondence,* p. 60); the reason he thought Drury Lane owed him money for the play is uncertain. A letter he wrote to Scott in July, 1817 (Constable Letter Book, National Library of Scotland MS 742, f. 139), mentions that Drury Lane acknowledges it owes him over £100 but cannot

pay the sum. Possibly the sum owing him would have arisen from the revival of *Bertram* (see n. 26).

32. Three previously unpublished Gothic scenes—one which stresses De Zelos's Gothic guilt, one in which Zimena relates a dream in which Alonzo had spoken to her, and one which contains Manuel's mad address to the corpses in his family vaults—appeared without any editorial comment in *New Monthly Magazine*, XI (April, 1819), 236–37. That these extracts appeared without any introductory material two years after *Manuel* failed attests the renown of Maturin in London.

33. *Examiner* (1817), 174.

34. *Monthly Review* (1817), 393.

35. *Scott-Maturin Correspondence*, pp. 91–92.

36. See Alaric Alfred Watts's biography of his father, *Alaric Watts: A Narrative of His Life* (London, 1884), I, 68–69. Only one review of this play has come to view, though the name of the paper that printed the review is not known; see Covent Garden, *Clippings from Newspapers*, Vol. II, 1789–1834; clipping dated May 16, 1819 (British Museum shelfmark Th.Cts. 39).

37. *Edinburgh Literary Journal*, III (April 24, 1830), 242–43; *Dublin Literary Gazette*, # 16 (April 17, 1830), pp. 244–46; *Irish Quarterly Review*, 166–69.

Chapter Four

1. Constable Letter Books, National Library of Scotland MS 790, f. 126; dated February 13, 1818. Constable also advised Maturin to change the original title, *De Courcy: Pour et Contre*, because *De Courcy* had already been used as a title; Constable Letter Books, National Library of Scotland MS 789, f. 829; dated August 8, 1817.

2. Maturin acceded to Scott's and Constable's advice, and wrote Scott that he burnt the manuscript; *Scott-Maturin Correspondence*, p. 89. But on August 27, 1818, he offered the preface to John Murray, to be published as a pamphlet (letter in the possession of John Murray, Ltd., of London), an offer Murray rejected. Acting against Scott's advice—indeed, behind his back in a fashion—indicates the financial strain Maturin was under.

3. Piper and Jeffares, "Maturin the Innovator," 278. Piper and Jeffares quote Alaric Watts, who calls the novel a "horrible anatomy of the moral frame" ("Memoir of the Rev. C. R. Maturin. (with a portrait)," *New Monthly Magazine*, XI [March, 1819], 167), evidently in reference to De Courcy's eventual apostasy and Zaira's powerful passion that lead them to elope.

4. *Edinburgh Review*, XXX (June, 1818), 252.

5. One wonders what Maturin meant when he wrote Scott that he was a "high Calvinist in my Religious opinions"; *Scott-Maturin Corres-*

pondence, p. 10. He evidently meant that he was a Trinitarian, as opposed to his "Unitarian Brethren," and a believer in predestination, as opposed to his "Armenian Masters" who held a more lenient view of man's control over his fate.

6. *Scott-Maturin Correspondence,* p. 82; Idman, p. 153.

7. Walter Scott likes *Women* because it does not have the ornament and luxuriousness of language of Maturin's earlier works; *Edinburgh Review,* 256. On the other hand, the reviewer in *The British Critic,* IX (June, 1818), 630–31, feels that even in *Women* Maturin is "perpetually overstretching himself for something beyond his grasp, and falling into bombast by an abuse of common language; like a fat man striding away on stilts, with his clothes made too tight for him." But this reviewer is objecting primarily to Maturin's "offences against sound grammar and good taste"—"Zaira visiting a convent, is described as 'holding herself down to the picture of the moral cancer of evil, eating into the core of life, and melting the fair face of things into a featureless and festering mass of corruption.'" Such offenses do not occur often in *Women,* however.

8. *Monthly Review,* CLXVII (August, 1818), 407–8; *Quarterly Review,* XIX (July, 1818), 322. Idman (p. 178) believes the vituperation in the *Quarterly Review* article attests to its being authored by John Wilson Croker, the notorious reviewer of Keats.

Chapter Five

1. "Memoranda of Maturin," *Douglas Jerrold's Shilling Magazine,* III (January, 1856), 132.

2. Constable Letter Books, National Library of Scotland MS 790, f. 639; dated September 9, 1819.

3. *Ibid.,* MS 791, f. 169; dated October 10, 1820.

4. Eino Railo, *The Haunted Castle: A Study of the Elements of English Romanticism* (London, 1927), p. 208.

5. See *London Magazine,* III (May, 1821), 518–19 n.

6. There is no explanation why almost all of Melmoth's activities take place in the seventeenth century. One can only assume that Maturin simply preferred to describe that century. There is no indication, certainly, that Melmoth's animosity toward humanity has lessened or his determination has flagged between the early stories and the adventures of Monçada, the only story with a contemporary setting.

7. Most of these, such as the description of the slow process of a vampire's sucking the blood of his victim and of the gambler father who has to endure the "speaking looks" of his hungry children, affect the late story, "The Tale of Guzman's Family." This part of *Melmoth* was written after *The Vampyre* was published in 1819, and after the earlier parts of *Melmoth* were already printed in sheets. But there is also one likely influence

of *The Vampyre* as early as "Stanton's Tale": Lord Ruthven (Polidori's vampire) leaving someone "formerly affluent . . . in the solitudes of a dungeon," an indication that almost all of the novel was written in late 1819 and 1820. This accords with the date of the letter in which a Constable editor chides Maturin for his tardiness (see n. 2 above).

8. Cp. Idman, p. 200; cf. Birkhead, p. 88.

9. I am only conjecturing that Maturin saw *Melmoth* as more than one tale. His publishers, confused by Maturin's erratic sending of manuscript, took the four volumes to be but one story. This idea was probably encouraged by the fact that the first story was named *Melmoth* by the printers while it was in press since Maturin had ignored numerous requests to send a title.

10. Maturin, *Five Sermons*, 2nd ed. (Dublin, 1826), p. 20.

11. Contemporary reviewers, no doubt wearied of Gothic settings, questioned whether even Maturin's views reflected reality; e.g., "Remarks on Maturin's Melmoth," *Scot's Magazine*, LXXXVII (May, 1821), 416; and (June, 1821), 537.

12. Francis Russell Hart, "The Experience of Character in the English Gothic Novels," *English Institute Essays* (New York, 1968), pp. 100–101, praises the documentation of Ambrosius' "psychological process."

13. In the "Preface" Maturin denies that "The Spaniard's Tale" is Radcliffean, but this part of it certainly is. Mario Praz has shown, further, that Maturin's use of the eighteenth-century theme of forced religious profession is taken—often with only translation from French to English— from Diderot's *La Religieuse; Review of English Studies*, VI (October, 1930), 429–36. A contemporary reviewer of *Universe* makes the same assertion concerning Alonzo's story; *Literary Gazette*, IX (June 9, 1821), 359.

14. So called because the order of Jesuits had been suspended in 1773.

15. W. Scholten, *Charles Robert Maturin: The Terror-Novelist* (Amsterdam, 1933), p. 100; see also *Edinburgh Review*, XXXV (July, 1821), 361.

16. "Remarks on 'Melmoth'," *New Monthly Magazine*, XIV (December, 1820), 663; *Monthly Review*, LXXV (January, 1821), 88.

17. Idman, p. 236.

18. *Ibid.*, p. 265. [John Wilson Croker], *Quarterly Review*, XXIV (January, 1821), 304–5; and Edgar Allan Poe in the introduction to his *Poems* of 1831 also question Maturin's method. Balzac in *Melmoth Reconcilié* (1835) and R. L. Stevenson in *The Bottle Imp* (1893) use Maturin's basic idea, but their "heroes" have no trouble in passing on the curse to criminals and drunkards. But the parricide probably would not take up Melmoth's proposal even were it made to him, although he concedes he has already "sealed those indentures here, which must be fulfilled below." The point is that his theology permits him to decrease his own suffering in the

hereafter by intensifying others' present physical suffering. The parricide is a thorough Manichean—in fact, he is more certain of the devil's existence than he is of God's. But he takes no chances.

19. The necessity for intellectual acquiescence does not alter the fact, as Idman (p. 265) points out, that Maturin's novel does not follow the principles of his sermon that the novel supposedly illustrates. "It is not the good instinct in the good [people], but the good instinct in the bad, which Maturin, in the preface, promises to demonstrate." The matter admittedly cannot be reconciled to Maturin's credit, in a purely logical sense; but Maturin conforms to a basic quality of Gothicism, the transience of effect and motive. Maturin selected for his preface a sermon passage that illustrated one religious concept; the novel itself, written under great pressure which was compounded by Constable's increasingly angry demands for the remainder of the manuscript, illustrates a different religious concept.

20. Idman, p. 265; William F. Axton, "Introduction" to *Melmoth the Wanderer* (Lincoln, Nebraska, 1961), p. xviii.

21. Charlotte Brontë, who was deeply read in Gothic literature, may have had this scene in mind when she wrote Rochester's proposal to Jane Eyre. The tree under which Rochester's proposal was made was split by lightning as a sign of nature's anger that Rochester should defy natural law by attempting bigamy.

22. See Idman (pp. 233–49) for a warmer appreciation of this tale.

23. *Ibid.,* pp. 236–37, explains the link between Immalee and Rousseau's Virginie. He also points out that Immalee's virtue contradicts Maturin's view, expressed in a sermon, that man in his natural state is brutal. But this brutality does not mean that Maturin opposes the Noble Savage theory; for, according to Rousseau, the stage of brutality in savages is the second, degenerate step toward civilization. Axton (p. xviii) prefers to call Immalee "the living presence of the undefiled religious impulse in mankind," rather than a "noble savage or a representative of natural goodness." But Axton does not develop this interesting idea. In fact, as stated by him the two descriptive phrases mean essentially the same; on this point, see also Hoxie Neale Fairchild, *The Noble Savage: A Study in Romantic Naturalism* (New York, 1928), pp. 381–84, 413–40.

24. Birkhead (p. 90) calls this "an uncommonly dull story."

25. Idman (p. 259) compares Elinor to Zaira; but Eva seems a more pertinent parallel.

26. The reason for this abruptness may be Constable's insistence that the novel be no longer than four volumes. The fourth volume, he said, was already too bulky: Constable Letter Books, National Library of Scotland, MS 791, ff. 95–96; dated July 10, 1820; and MS 791, f. 102; dated July 24, 1820.

Chapter Six

1. Perhaps his health delayed the completion of *The Albigenses,* as it had *Melmoth.* The novel was originally scheduled for publication in the spring of 1822; see *Scott-Maturin Correspondence,* p. 99. But no biographical data survives for this period of Maturin's life.

2. Published as *Five Sermons of the Errors of the Roman Catholic Church* (Dublin and London, 1824).

3. Maturin's last recorded duty was a baptism on August 8. He died on October 30, and was buried on November 2, 1824, in St. Peter's churchyard.

4. This history of the Albigenses is taken from Hoffman Nickerson, *The Inquisition: A Political and Military Study of its Establishment* (Boston, 1923); A. L. Maycock, *The Inquisition: From its Establishment to the Great Schism* (New York, 1927); "Cathari," *Encyclopedia Britannica* (Chicago, 1963), V, 71–72; and "Albigenses," *Encyclopedia Americana* (New York, 1964), I, 337–38. Because primary documents written by the Albigenses were destroyed by the order of the Inquisition established by Pope Innocent, the beliefs of the Cathari have to be conjectured from the statements of the victorious papal supporters.

5. On the other hand, two of the Catholics seem to be practicing Manicheans. The Lord of Courtenaye longs to see the Devil; he employs a number of witches and implores Marie de Mortemar to help him achieve his goal. The Bishop of Toulouse distinguishes between the powers of God and of Satan in a speech to Genevieve that I refer to later in the text. But whether Maturin uses this material ironically and humorously, or satirically, toward the Roman Catholic church is not clear; for he does not develop the matter beyond these scenes.

Selected Bibliography

PRIMARY WORKS

1. Novels

Fatal Revenge; or, The Family of Montorio: A Romance. By Dennis Jasper Murphy [pseudonym]. London: Longman, Hurst, Rees, and Orme, 1807.

The Wild Irish Boy. London: Longman, Hurst, Rees, and Orme, 1808.

The Milesian Chief: A Romance. London: Henry Colburn, 1812.

Women: or, Pour et Contre. Edinburgh: Constable and Company, 1818; London: Longman, Hurst, Rees, and Orme, 1818.

Melmoth the Wanderer: A Tale. Edinburgh: Constable and Company, 1820; London: Hurst, Robinson, and Co., 1820.

The Albigenses: A Romance. London: Hurst, Robinson, and Co., 1824; Edinburgh: Constable and Company, 1824.

2. Plays

Bertram; or, The Castle of St. Aldobrand: A Tragedy. London: John Murray, 1816.

Manuel: A Tragedy. London: John Murray, 1817.

Fredolfo: A Tragedy. London: Longman, Hurst, Rees, Orme, and Brown, 1819; and Hurst, Robinson, and Co., 1819; Edinburgh: Archibald Constable and Co., 1819.

"Osmyn, the Renegade; or, The Siege of Salerno: A Tragedy." [Unpublished; excerpts printed in *The Edinburgh Literary Journal,* III (April 24, 1830), 242–43.]

3. Sermons

Sermons. Edinburgh: Archibald Constable and Co., 1819; London: Longman, Hurst, Rees, Orme, and Brown, 1819; and Hurst, Robinson, and Co., 1819. Written on a variety of subjects. The correspondence that survives between Maturin and Constable (in the National Library of Scotland) indicates that Maturin experienced considerable difficulty in collecting enough sermons to make a full volume.

Five Sermons of the Errors of the Roman Catholic Church. 2nd ed. Dublin: William Curry, Jun. & Co., 1826; London: Hamilton, Adams, and Co., 1826. [First edition, 1824.] The sermons reveal Maturin as a dedicated and even hortatory preacher, but one whose theological opinions could be confused.

156

4. *Essays*

"*The Apostate:* a Tragedy, in Five Acts. by Richard Sheil." *Quarterly Review,* XVII (April, 1817), 248–60.

"*Harrington and Ormond, Tales.* By Maria Edgeworth." *The British Review, and London Critical Journal,* XI (February, 1818), 37–61. The esthetic ideas in Maturin's surveys of the histories of the drama and the novel do not always accord with his own practice. The essays were published anonymously; Maturin's authorship is stated in his correspondence with Sir Walter Scott and the publisher, John Murray.

5. *Poems*

Lines on the Battle of Waterloo. Dublin: R. Milliken, 1816. The 1815 prize poem at Trinity College, Dublin. Attributed to Maturin by his anonymous biographer in *New Monthly Magazine,* XIX (May, 1827), 406; but published under the authorship of John Shee, a Trinity College undergraduate to whom Maturin is supposed to have given the copyright. The poem has a few Maturin-like qualities, but they are too general to enable one to definitely ascribe the work to him. Such qualities are the imagery (a pile of dying soldiers called a "*human hill*"); frequent allusions to religion and the moral lessons to be learned from Napoleon's fall; and frequent references to Irish harps and to Wellington as a "son of the green Isle." The notes have a modest and unstrained wit in their defence against an anticipated charge of plagiarism.

The Universe: A Poem. London: Henry Colburn, 1821. This work has Maturin's name on the title page, and he may have written parts of it, but his authorship of the whole is doubtful. The sons of the Reverend James Mills claimed that their father had written the poem and that he had allowed Maturin to publish it because Maturin could not think of a subject and had already spent the publisher's advance; see *Notes & Queries,* series 5, II (1874), 428 [November 28]; III (1875), 20 [January 2], 172–73 [February 27], 240 [March 20], 280 [April 3], and 340 [April 24]. On the other hand, Maturin claimed to have written the poem in 1813 and to have sent the manuscript to Colburn in a period of great financial distress after the Constable firm had declined to publish it. In either case, the poem merits little attention. Loosely modelled on the eighteenth-century physio-theological poem, its principal qualities are flowery turgidity and abstractness. What interest it has lies in the doubts its publishing history has raised about Maturin's character.

6. *Posthumous Fragments*

"Leixlip Castle: An Irish Family Legend." *The Literary Souvenir; or,*

Cabinet of Poetry and Romance. London: Hurst, Robinson, and Co.,
    1825. Pp. 211–32.
"The Sybil's Prophecy: A Dramatic Fragment." *The Literary Souvenir;
    or, Cabinet of Poetry and Romance.* London: Hurst, Robinson, and
    Co., 1826. Pp. 128–36.

7. Manuscripts and Letters

"Bertram." The original manuscript version. In Abbotsford, Sir Walter
    Scott's home.
Letters to John Murray, the London publisher. In the offices of John
    Murray, Ltd., London.
Letters to Archibald Constable, the Edinburgh publisher; and copies of
    letters from Constable to Maturin. In the Constable Letter Books,
    now in the National Library of Scotland, Edinburgh.
Ratchford, Fannie E., and William H. McCarthy, Jr., eds. *The Cor-
    respondence of Sir Walter Scott and Charles Robert Maturin.* Austin:
    University of Texas Press, 1937. Invaluable source of biographical
    details. Letters reveal Maturin as impecunious if well-meaning and as
    somewhat demanding on Scott's powers of patronage and recom-
    mendation. Excellent editors' notes.

Secondary Sources

1. Biography

"Memoir of Charles Robert Maturin." *Melmoth the Wanderer:* A New
    Edition from the Original Text. London: Richard Bentley & Son,
    1892. The preparation of this memoir was supposedly assisted in by
    Maturin's descendants, including his grandnephew, Oscar Wilde. The
    introductory material also contains a critical note on Maturin and
    a bibliography of Maturin's works and of reviews of his works. In
    all, a useful body of material.
New Monthly Magazine. "Conversations of Maturin." XIX (May, 1827),
    401–11; XIX (June, 1827), 571–77. "Recollections of Maturin," XX
    (August, 1827), 146–52; XX (October, 1827), 370–76. Most of the
    later biographies can be traced back to this series of repetitious
    reminiscences purportedly by a close acquaintance. Contains some
    interesting dialogue in which Maturin expresses his opinion on sundry
    topics; but, on the whole, it gives only an external view of his character.

2. Gothicism and Critical Studies

Axton, William F. "Introduction" to *Melmoth.* Lincoln: University of
    Nebraska Press, 1961. Impressive summary of Gothicism. Perceptive
    if sometimes sophistical comments on *Melmoth.*
Bailey, J. O. "Introduction." *British Plays of the Nineteenth Century: An*

Anthology to Illustrate the Evolution of the Drama. New York; Odyssey Press, Inc., 1966. Pp. 1–38. Brief but cogent presentation of the eighteenth-century theater influence upon nineteenth-century plays and actors.

BAKER, DONALD WHITELAW. "Themes of Terror in Nineteenth Century English Fiction: The Shift to the Internal." Unpublished Ph.D. dissertation; Brown University, 1955. Has an excellent survey of Gothicism from the eighteenth century through the early twentieth century. Nonclinical psychopathology.

BAKER, ERNEST A. *The History of the English Novel. V: The Novel of Sentiment and the Gothic Romance.* London: H. F. & G. Witherby, Ltd., 1929. Accurate details and unexciting commentary.

BIRKHEAD, EDITH. *The Tale of Terror: A Study of the Gothic Romance.* London: Constable & Company, Ltd., 1921; New York: Russell & Russell, Inc., 1963. Supercilious comments on *Melmoth;* some gross errors of fact; but generous view of Maturin's worth.

CLARK, KENNETH. *The Gothic Revival: An Essay in the History of Taste.* New York: Charles Scribner's Sons, 1929. On architecture as the first element in creating the eighteenth-century interest in the Gothic.

DAWSON, LEVEN M. *"Melmoth the Wanderer:* Paradox and the Gothic Novel." *Studies in English Literature,* VIII (Autumn, 1968), 621–32. Excellent study of the operation of paradox in Gothicism.

EVANS, BERTRAND. *Gothic Drama from Walpole to Shelley.* Berkeley and Los Angeles: University of California Press, 1947. University of California Publications in English, Vol. 18. Indispensable; still the only full-length study of Gothic drama. Incisive and clear tracing of the genre's development and its evolution toward Romantic drama.

———. "Manfred's Remorse and Dramatic Tradition," *Publications of the Modern Language Association,* LXII (1947), 752–73. On the Byronic-Gothic hero-villain.

FAIRCHILD, HOXIE NEALE. *The Noble Savage: A Study in Romantic Naturalism.* New York: Columbia University Press, 1928. Level-headed survey of this important motif of sensibility.

FLANAGAN, THOMAS. *The Irish Novelists: 1800–1850.* New York: Columbia University Press, 1959. Sections on Maria Edgeworth and Lady Morgan have relevance to Maturin's efforts to imitate these ladies' successes.

FOSTER, JAMES R. *History of the Pre-Romantic Novel in England.* New York: Modern Language Association; London: Oxford University Press; 1949. Detailed, rational survey concluding with the work of Ann Radcliffe.

FRYE, NORTHROP. "The Drunken Boat: The Revolutionary Element in Romanticism." *Romanticism Reconsidered: Selected Papers from the English Institute.* Ed. Northrop Frye. New York & London: Columbia

University Press, 1963. Pp. 1–25. Excellent discussion of Romanticism; many of the qualities isolated by Frye are also present in Gothicism.

GAER, JOSEPH. *The Legend of the Wandering Jew.* New York: New American Library (Mentor Book), 1961. Informal but informative.

HART, FRANCIS RUSSELL. "The Experience of Character in the English Gothic Novel." *Experience in the Novel: Selected Papers from the English Institute.* Ed. Roy Harvey Pearce. New York & London: Columbia University Press, 1968. Pp. 83–105. Useful summary of possible perspectives on reality in Gothic fiction. Argues that Gothic (symbolic) literature also has a level of psychological mimesis that must be taken into account in critical judgments, a view especially relevant to *Melmoth.*

HEILMAN, ROBERT B. "Charlotte Brontë's 'New' Gothic." *From Jane Austen to Joseph Conrad: Essays Collected in Memory of James T. Hillhouse.* Eds. Robert C. Rathburn and Martin Steinmann, Jr. Minneapolis: University of Minnesota Press, 1958. Pp. 118–32. Important essay on the nature of Gothic literature. Gothicism employs "extra-rationality" to "enlarge the sense of reality."

HINCK, HENRY WILLIAM. "Three Studies in Charles Robert Maturin." Unpublished Ph.D. dissertation; State University of Iowa, 1954. Mainly a detailed study of *Bertram;* has a generally sound analysis of the play's faults, strengths, and sources.

IDMAN, NIILO. *Charles Robert Maturin: His Life and Works.* London: Constable & Co., Ltd., 1923. Excellent full-length study of Maturin; thoroughly researched in contemporary reviews and biography. Valuable for its analysis of Maturin's borrowings and influences. Has long plot summaries and judicious if limited critical comments.

LOVEJOY, ARTHUR O. "The First Gothic Revival, and the Return to Nature," *Modern Language Notes,* XLVII (November, 1932), 419–46. Study of nature and architecture.

NELSON, LOWRY, JR. "Night Thoughts on the Gothic Novel," *Yale Review,* n.s. LII (Winter, 1963), 236–57. Widely theoretical tracing of the ambiguity of good and evil in Gothic literature. Nothing on Maturin directly.

NICKERSON, HOFFMAN. *The Inquisition: A Political and Military Study of its Establishment.* Boston and Now York: Houghton Mifflin, 1923. Excellent detail and interpretation; deals primarily with the Albigensian heresy and the Albigensian Crusade.

NICOLL, ALLARDYCE. *A History of English Drama 1660–1900. IV: Early Nineteenth Century Drama 1800–1850.* Cambridge, England: University of Cambridge Press, 1955. Comprehensive study of the audience and theaters and of the different genres of drama. Includes extensive bibliography of plays produced.

PENZOLDT, PETER. *The Supernatural in Fiction.* London: Peter Nevill, 1952. Fascinating psychoanalytical study of the modern "weird" short story, with a few references to the traditional Gothic writers.

PIPER, H.W., and A. NORMAN JEFFARES. "Maturin the Innovator," *Huntington Library Quarterly,* XII (1958), 261–84. Restrained but sound analysis of Maturin's use of Irish nationalism in his novels, and his reaction to Wordsworthian idealism.

PRAZ, MARIO. *The Romantic Agony.* Trans. Angus Davidson. London: Oxford University Press, 1933; New York: Meridian Books, 1956. Survey of erotic sensibility. Especially relevant to Maturin by showing context of Maturin's interest in suffering.

RAILO, EINO. *The Haunted Castle: A Study of the Elements of English Romanticism.* London: George Routledge & Sons, Ltd.; New York: E. P. Dutton & Co., 1927. Studies of the Wandering Jew and other motifs in Gothic fiction.

SCHOLTEN, W. *Charles Robert Maturin: The Terror-Novelist.* Amsterdam: H. J. Paris, 1933. An extremely uneven book. Has some value for its noting of reviews.

SUMMERS, MONTAGUE. *A Gothic Bibliography.* London: Fortune Press, 1941; New York: Russell & Russell, Inc., 1964. Standard bibliography. Also includes non-Gothic works by "Gothic" writers.

——— *The Gothic Quest: A History of the Gothic Novel.* London: Fortune Press, 1938; New York: Russell & Russell, Inc., 1964. Rich with facts.

TARR, SISTER MARY MURIEL. *Catholicism in Gothic Fiction: A Study of the Nature and Function of Catholic Materials in Gothic Fiction in England (1762–1820).* Washington, D.C.: Catholic University of America Press, 1956. Demonstrates that most writers used Catholicism for its emotional and dramatic effect but were not necessarily opposed to actual Catholic practices and doctrines, about which they often were mistaken.

TOMPKINS, J. M. S. *The Popular Novel in England, 1770–1800.* London: Constable & Company, Ltd., 1932. Important survey that relates the Gothic novel to its contemporary literary background.

VARMA, DEVENDRA P. *The Gothic Flame.* London: Arthur Barker, Ltd., 1957. Best survey of Gothic developments. Also has excellent quotations from the novels, but these are sometimes introduced with insufficient critical commentary. Has useful bibliography. Brief but pertinent appendix compares Gothic novels to modern detective novels.

Index